# LOVING THE GODDESS WITHIN

# LOVING THE GODDESS WITHIN

## Sex Magick for Women

# NAN HAWTHORNE

delphi
press

Delphi Press, Inc., Oak Park, Illinois

96 95 94 93 92 91  5 4 3 2 1


ISBN 0-878980-01-7

Library of Congress Catalogue Card Number 90-86176


The paper used in this publication meets the minimum requirements of American National Standard for Information Sciences—Permanence of Paper for Printed Library Materials, ANSI Z39.48-1984.

The text of this book is printed on recycled paper.


Photography by Ted Lacey

*I want to thank all those who have encouraged and supported me through-out the formulation of my ideas and the writing of this book, especially the members of the Circles of Exchange who have given me so much joy and such a sense of purpose these past years.*

*I dedicate this book to Jim, whose awareness of the Goddess in himself as well as in me, unflagging feminism and tender love and friendship nurture and inspire me.*

# Contents

# Introduction: Loving the Goddess Within

Put aside the big books now, the books on ceremonial Witchcraft, the intricate works on ritual crafting, spells and incantations, the profound books on techniques to mesh your magickal and daily life. They are all important and will leave you enriched beyond your expectations, and you may read them later. But for now it's time to play. The Goddess inside of you, the Goddess Who IS you, wants to sink into a hot tub up to her neck in musky suds, to laugh with a playmate, to nibble a sweet, and to trail imaginary wisps of stars in the air with the tips of her toes.

This book has a heavy purpose, to bring forth from you the love for the Goddess which is the love for yourself. It has a tall task, since you were raised to believe your body's desires were at worst shameful or at best rather trivial. But in each of us is the giggling girl-child who likes nothing better than to swirl her tongue through rich, sweet ice cream, to run just as fast as she can through a field of tall grass, to snuggle up in a flannel nightgown straight out of the dryer on a cold night, or to thrust both hands up to the wrist in cool, slippery mud pies.

But it is not a heavy book. There are no stern admonitions or daunting rhetoric. With very little encouragement from me, you are going to have some fun, and, if you keep doing it, you'll find the Goddess freed within you. And She'll thank us both for it. In this book you will find some exploration of where all the "body negative" messages came from, why we as women stopped dancing, our bodies painted with lewd and joyful symbols, why we came to believe we didn't like sex but only bore it for "his needs," and why we now crowd into psychologists' offices and diet centers alike to work off the same low self esteem. You'll learn how basic and functional sexual symbolism is in a world where billions upon billions of creatures are reproducing themselves every moment, and how these symbols can enhance your understanding of and enjoyment of magick. You will gain some tools for healing that part of your life that longs for affirmation by applying that vibrant sense of magick to your love of your own and others' bodies. And you'll start thinking of how we might gift our daughters and their daughters with a tide of love and pleasure so revolutionary that patriarchy may just collapse of its own sour paleness.

In gratitude to the Goddess for the wonder and pleasure of my own life, I offer this playbook to my sisters.

Nan Hawthorne
Seattle, Washington
*February 1990*

# 1

## The Goddess's Gift

Love and sex are essential parts of magick, being the re-enactments of the Goddess's initiating and sustaining energy and of the cycles of fertility. Magick itself is a creative concept, being defined as the drawing in of power, from the deity or various Earthly celestial energies and the reshaping of that power into an altered form. Early humans, whose lives were spent in constant awareness of natural cycles, knew that the energy of sexuality and childbirth was part of the workings of the natural world that included them. Their first observation was the similarity of gestation with the turning of the year. They noticed that the young of animals appeared at certain times of the year and that, even in more southerly climates, plants tended to put up shoots after a seeming dormant period. Each year there was a time of renewal of the very source of their survival, their food and the fuel for their fires. The growth of a child within a woman's body is preceded by the dormancy of her menses. The invisible infant eventually coming forth, blooming, followed the pattern observed in nature every day and all around.

The step from the comparison to recognizing the symbolism of the Earth as a Great Mother was, quite literally, natural. Women were revered as the inheritors of the Mother's ability to create life. Men's role in procreation was not as apparent, and the attraction that women held for most men was seen as a pull towards that procreative power. The physical distinctness of the genders, the penis which enlarged in union and the vagina and breasts as both the seats of pleasure for a woman and the organs for birth and nurturance of a child, galvanized the bond between them in the magick of fertility. Ancient cave paintings and artifacts frequently represent women or more specifically Goddesses with exaggerated breasts, bellies, and vulvas, while male figures have huge phalluses. The religion of the Goddess was born as a fertility religion.

Early people constantly observed connections between their own actions and the changes in their world. They believed that through recognizing and honoring these connections they could enhance their survival. The Goddess and her partners expected and approved certain constructive behavior and liked to see human recognition and celebration of Her. Communal benefit and caring for the natural environment provided social codes. Seasonal manifestations such as weather changes, moon phases and the sun's position became occasions to gather together to propitiate the divinities with rituals, dance and drama representing myths full of sex and the symbols of the Earth's and human fertility. People painted what they wanted to happen, such as successful hunts, and carved fertility figures to arouse the interest of the Goddess and God. There was no disassociation of themselves from the natural and thus of their own fertility from that of the Great Mother.

Since the symbolism of the seed and semen took some time to emerge, sex was more than just a magickal act to urge deities to bless the hunt. People enjoyed it. Just as fire and warm furs soothed the chilled body and food filled the aching emptiness of the belly and gave strength, sexual desire, pleasure and release satisfied and comforted the body. Attraction drew people together, created bonds, provided a complement that was mutually beneficial. Again the connection was inevitable:

Mother Earth provided the materials for warmth, shelter, and food, and granted to women the ability to create life. Certainly this other satisfaction was likewise Her gift.

Ancient creation stories feature initiating and creating Goddesses who gave birth to the universe or Earth joyfully or shaped them with loving and artistically fertile hands. Australia's Eingana the All-Creating was the sea and originally vomited her creations onto the Earth. Finding herself unhappy with this rather inconvenient method, she swallowed everything she had hitherto created, filling herself so that her belly bulged and bulged until, seeing her discomfort, the sky God, her lover, pierced her near her anus with his phallic spear so that all the creatures could spill forth through the newly made birth canal. Together, Eingana and her lover invented the vagina and intercourse.

The Panamanian Earth Mother, Mu Olokukurtilisop, gave birth first to the sun and, immediately taken with her beautiful new child, made love to him. She then gave birth to her grandson, the moon, and was so aroused by him that she made love with him thousands of times to create the stars. Mu, so rich in her joy in making love, mated with each and every star enough times to create all the living things of the Earth from her teeming womb.

The Southwest Native American Spider Woman wove a web that connected the four quarters, east, south, west and north, and gave birth to two daughters. The daughters fashioned the sun and moon and became the ancient mothers of the Earth's people, whom Spider Woman fashioned lovingly for them out of red, yellow, black and white clay.

Mawu, the all-creator of the Dahomey people of Africa, fashioned the world riding on the back of a great serpent, its undulations creating valleys and mountains. Afterwards she asked her serpent friend to coil up below the surface of the Earth to help it bear the weight of all the trees, lions, zebras, humans, and other plants and animals she herself had fashioned.

Ancient mythology abounds with similar tales of the All-Mother creating with love, artistic skill and vibrant sexuality, often alone, sometimes sharing the act of creation with sisters or daughters, and sometimes revealing the first glimmerings of understanding of the role of the male in procreation.

## Priestesses and Whores

The development of agriculture and the domestication of animals provided the first hint of the male role in reproduction. Women's intricate involvement in these advances strengthened their identification with a bounteous Mother Earth, and the new idea of a connection between sex and pregnancy further intensified the magickal symbolism of sex. In many cultures the role of the holy woman or priestess involved some celebration of the Goddess through the pleasure of the body. Now sexual union as an imitation of the Goddess's initiatory and creative power provided even greater magickal symbolism. The act of intercourse itself or its imagery in ritual propitiated the deities for abundance at harvest time. The priestess's role as human representative of the Goddess included lovemaking, and as cities developed and temples were built, these women chose lovers from among the people to honor the Mother. Thereby her own primal energy grew, and those she chose were blessed with bountiful farms or successful trade. Men came to seek out the temple "prostitutes" in order to gain the Goddess's blessing, providing gifts of food or the tools of living to the temple in payment for it. In return, they were cleansed of masculine habits, such as war, and brought to the Goddess again. The Sumerian word for temple prostitute was Quedishtu, "the undefiled one," to whom the man stained by killing could come to be rededicated to life. This practice lives on in our deep unconscious, as soldiers flock to prostitutes while on leave, to reaffirm life and to drown visions of horror in the smiling, laughing vitality of a woman. The Goddess continues to be served.

But as these societies developed, the role of the male in conception became evident, then preeminent, and a new problem was invented. Human parentage had always been clear: everyone knew out of whose body a child had come, who was the mother. Family tradition, relationships, tribal position and property were matrifocal: based on the relationship of mother and child. The number of sexual partners a woman had was simply irrelevant. When men came to know that they were in fact far from irrelevant in procreation, the problem of identifying a man's children preoccupied them. The only way to know for sure who was your child was to prevent your mate or mates from having intercourse with any other men. As patrifocal societies developed, female sexual fidelity was intrinsic to maintaining position and property. So long as the God was the Goddess's son and under Her care or control, men could not control their mates. Nor could they if she was equal. So first Goddesses were subjugated, then ultimately purged from religion. As always men were made in the image of God, but now the God, in men's patriarchal image, dominated, and women became a poor imitation of the God and His favored ones. In the myths women became an afterthought, the "assistant" or slave to men and subject to his commands or, if they rebelled, harridans and "Witches."

These patrifocal cultures existed in some places side by side with others that still honored the Goddess. These new societies were unable to live in peace with the matrifocal communities. They went to war armed with religious intolerance in addition to swords and spears. They called the temple priestesses "whores" and named their practices demeaning and an "abomination."

Because all women in these societies could serve as stand-ins for the fertility Goddesses and so could act as priestesses, this made the intercessionary role of the patriarchal priests redundant and women became a danger to their positions in society. Women were a threat wherever they had power over their own sexuality. Sexual violence was not only condoned but was approved as an antidote to women's attempt to "usurp" the power granted by God to men. Menstrual huts had been the sacred meeting places of women, so powerful from the sacred bloods women shared with the Goddess as the sign of creation and divinity, that they were off limits to all men. The huts now became taboo places, "unclean," and menstruation itself was forcibly transformed by envious men into a "curse," to be despised and avoided at all costs.

So long as the attraction of men to women existed, however, men feared their own need. In their efforts to expunge the female deity and Her role as the fertile Earth Mother, they were forced to repress sexuality itself. The resentment and polarity between the sexes intensified. In both the West and East patriarchal societies grew and the norm became one in which the only pure love was defined as that which denied the physical. Even men themselves, unwilling and unable to resist their sexual needs, twisted their natural urges into sources for guilt or often violence, culminating in Western culture in the extreme prudishness and pain known as the Victorian Era.

### We Reclaim Our Bodies

Okay, that's how repression developed. But what of today? The Victorian Era, and all the centuries of sexual repression prior to it, is over, right?. Sex is becoming an acceptable subject for conversation, within limits. In some places and by some people, sexual self-determination is tolerated although not generally encouraged. Women have relearned the orgasm, or at least have been reminded or allowed to insist that it exists. Clearly whatever one tries to say about sex in a contemporary context is hemmed in by conditions or restrictions.

Although the patriarchal interests exemplified by Victorian sexual repression are not quite ready to loose their hold on our psyches just yet, the twentieth century has seen a somewhat superficial shift in the West's attitude toward sex. Psychologists and biologists have adopted physical intimacy from its former caretakers, the churches. But even though we have inherited the benefit of a fresh look at sex, of a wider and more informed consideration of it, the materialist approach of these scientists has precluded the eradication of the true shackles on healthy sexual expression. Instead of liberating us, most of the various liberalizing movements of this century have only managed to twist these shackles to their own purposes. We have been left tantalized with a promise but are still unable or not allowed to find the freedom we seek.

It would also be a mistake to assume that patriarchal religions have given up their power over attitudes about sexuality. Not only do Christian denominations such as the Roman Catholic Church preserve control over such sexual issues as premarital sex and adultery, birth control, abortion, and divorce, the upsurge of the New Fundamentalism reclaimed its perceived right to dictate on these issues and more, including censorship of sexually explicit materials and sex education for children. These churches persist in proclaiming the essentially subjugated role of women, denying them simple control over their own bodies. Fewer people seem willing to permit these churches to dictate sexual mores on a legislative level. Still their political power can be dominating and the nagging inference that sex is somehow "bad" lingers in our psyches.

Ironically, these same Fundamentalist churches warn of the danger of New Age religions, which in reality preach much the same message of disassociation of spirit and body. Even those

New Age groups that are beginning to find benefit in empowering the female often do so using images of passivity and compliance, failing to discover the wholeness of a woman. They teach the denial of the body, through fasting or celibacy, to heighten the spiritual, which is represented as "higher." Many deny the role of the physical world altogether, finding the source for all reality in the spiritual alone, thereby creating the concept that illness or injury is not the result of microbes or accident but of one's own maladjusted spritual enlightenment. These concepts reveal themselves as typical of patriarchal religion. (The similarity of language between many New Age groups and Goddess religion must not be confused as similarity of basic beliefs.)

There are many different schools of clinical and popular psychology, and, even if some do encourage individuals to express their own sexuality, it is popular culture, a synthesis of unrelated and often contradictory themes from various sources, which holds sway over most of us. Whereas we formerly might have fretted over whether or not an aspect of sex was sinful, we are now more likely to worry about how healthy or well-balanced it is. For example, while an individual may not believe that to masturbate is to break the law of God, she may worry that she is masturbating too much and may be obsessed with it, or that once she is in a sexual relationship she should stop wanting to masturbate.

The so-called sexual liberation of the 1960s brought women a whole new set of constraints. Sex was deemed by the youth culture to be a free expression, but the woman in these "free" relationships was given a mixed message. She was expected to comply with the sexual demands of men or be labeled "hung up." And the liberation was the sole province of heterosexuals. Gay men and lesbians were little tolerated and sometimes the object of rancor or violence by members of the Peace Generation who considered them the products of a decadent society.

Concurrently the "establishment" had its own sexual liberation, with fashions in clothing and lifestyle becoming more provocative or sophisticated, yet with the same sexual double-bind for women. It was partly this heritage of repression by the Father Church tortured into new shapes by the scientific community and then the hippie and *Playboy* mentality that sparked both the Gay/Lesbian and Women's Liberation Movements. While the former has managed to keep alive many issues of the freedom of sexual self-expression in spite of the renewed homophobia arising from the New Fundamentalism and their exploitation of AIDS paranoia, the initial burst of sexual exploration by the Women's Movement has lost steam. In the early 1970s there was an outpouring of interest in women's sexuality, with books on masturbation, lesbian relationships, help for preorgasmic women, and the reassessment of concepts of beauty in body image and clothing. The Women's Movement continues to dedicate energy to reproductive rights and the struggle for legislative reform on rape and physical abuse of women and children. However, perhaps because a hint of Victorian mores persists, the positive emphasis on women's sexuality has recently taken a seat further back, and now there is conflict within the Women's Movement over the different perceptions of the nature of sexual expression, such as in sexually explicit entertainment.

## We Reclaim the Goddess

The modern reconsideration and exploration of Witchcraft as the great-grand daughter of the ancient Goddess religion by such authors as Margaret Murray, Z. Budapest, Merlin Stone, Starhawk and others, and the growing concern for the preservation of our natural environment have linked with feminism and energized a return to the Goddess. This is the opportunity for all of us to dredge up from our psyches the affirmation of own sexuality. We can reject the bonds inherent in all patriarchal structures, whether religious, social, or scientific, and return to both women and men the deep satisfaction of union with natural cycles and spirituality.

Witchcraft, particularly what feminists refer to as Dianic Witchcraft, is generally viewed by its adherents as the descendant of those ancient Goddess traditions, the traditions of fertility and creativity, of recognition of our part in the natural world that we revere. Far from condoning domination and violence, it is a religion of personal responsibility and self-reliance. Its traditions and ritual are rich with attunement to natural rhythms and a simple joyousness and vitality.

In Witchcraft we still recognize the gifts of the Goddess. While few of us now grow our own food, and fewer still hunt for meat or furs and scrounge for wood for shelters or fire, we are not ignorant of nor ungrateful for the food and energy with which She supplies us. We have the added benefit of recognizing the intricate complexities of life in the universe. Wonder is intensified rather than lessened by further understanding and learning. We have long known of the connection between intercourse and conception. We may therefore synthesize the ancient symbols of fertility with the creation myths of the burgeoning patriarchal societies to fabricate new creation stories. These stories can be full of honor for the Mother and symbols of the link between sex and the creation of life. Further, with the rejection of patriarchal taboos, we need no longer limit our pleasures to only those that might possibly end in conception, but can glory in the psychic and emotional creative energy of love-making of all kinds: masturbation, same gender relationships, and multiple relationships in addition to heterosexual pair-bonding.

Sex in one's magickal life can intensify one's understanding of the elemental nature of the Earth. Sometimes, in our concrete towns and cities, riding around in our fossil-fueled metal conveyances, it is difficult to be attuned to what the Earth is doing. We heat ourselves when it's cold, cool ourselves when it's hot. We transport exotic foods to our tables. We supplement the Earth's bounty with chemical vitamins and sun lamps. We holiday in the summer, when earlier cultures were busiest, and work during the natural hibernation time. For some the only natural sight may be a petunia in a window box. To remedy this, Witches endeavor to inject more of the natural world into our lives. We do this by removing some of the artificiality and replacing it with nature's gifts. We use the symbols of air, fire, water, Earth and spirit, of celestial bodies and their positions, of various aspects and names of the Goddess and God aligned with certain seasons or items in the environment. And we ritualize observance of the Earth's cycles through the seasonal sabbats and the celebration of the lunar phases. We can use sex and the symbols of sex to bring further connection with the Earth's cycle of fertility. We can empower ourselves and our magickal practice with this reclaimed energy.

The Goddess's gift can go further than the enhancement of Her rituals and craft. Magick in one's sex life can lend spontaneity and joy and release one from patriarchal restrictions. With a recognition of the essence of sex in observance of the Mother's cycles, new light is shed on the negative power of patriarchal religions. "Dominion over the Earth" was Jehovah's gift to Adam. By dominating sex he controlled the Earth, and vice versa. To stifle one is to stifle the other. Witches are among those who see a necessary end to manipulating and stifling Earth's fertility.

Denying free expression of that other gift, the pleasure of love-making, is as destructive to the individual and to the combined psychic energy of all. We become more self-destructive, more estranged from one another. To reclaim the Goddess in our own bodies and its pleasures is to set out on the path toward both self-nourishment and universal harmony. On the way to making love, not war, we may find Her gift liberating within us the fertility of self-love, mutual connection and understanding. When we say no to paternalistic boundaries against self-love and empowerment and their loving exchange with the partners of our own choosing, we liberate ourselves to become adventurous and fulfilled in our own pleasures. Symbols are keys to empowerment, and the symbols of Witchcraft are full of the Goddess and her fertile world.

## Women Loving . . .

This book is intended for women who are learning to love the special physical/spiritual aspect of the Goddess. It recognizes that there is a diversity in its readers and therefore a diversity in focus and opportunities. There will be women alone, women in relationships with other women, and women in relationships with men. Most of the exercises, meditations, and rituals are written entirely with feminine pronouns. However, there is no assumption made that only women in relationships with women will use this book. In fact, for me to have achieved my goal in writing the book any person, female or male, should find growth, self-regard, and a key to one aspect of the Goddess available to her/him. Where a character or pronoun gives you trouble, change it. Or try to find the female or male aspects represented in each person. Being alone should not preclude use of the book either, as you can find the "others" represented within yourself, either through fantasies or as actual other yous.

## . . . Women

Plato tells a beautiful story about love and sex in his dialogue *The Symposium*: once upon a time all of us were matched in pairs, our bodies attached at the back. The wrath of a God was unleashed as a terrible lightning bolt that split us all apart and sent each of us somersaulting through time and space alone. Grief-stricken by the loss of our twin, we each spend our many lives searching for that other. Those pairs who were a woman and a man are heterosexual. Those who were two men are gay men. And those who were two women are lesbians.

In another way women who seek out another woman to love are searching for their twin, for the Goddess's part in humans is most readily apparent in women. But women must first recognize the Goddess in themselves alone. This is more convenient because we are always physically available to ourselves. Yet loving ourselves, being in love with ourselves, is difficult for most of us. We are raised to believe that women are other-directed. Our society, our families, our churches, many of our psychologists, and our popular culture drum this into little girls' minds and never let up. Further, any vestigial fondness for ourselves or our bodies is stripped away by a culture that imposes impossible standards for appearance and behavior on its females. I originally decided to write this book after years of listening to women, feminists and even some Witches, berate themselves for real and imagined "defects" in appearance and behavior. Nowhere will you find among men the extent of self-repugnance and self-reproach that you find among women. How can we love the Goddess's image in ourselves if we are convinced that we are unloveable and undesirable?

The first place to look for and desire the Goddess is in yourself. In a later chapter I will suggest ways of first finding yourself attractive and then learning to make love to yourself. Almost all of us masturbate. It's a hush-hush practice, but the need for sexual release is so strong that even women who find the idea uncomfortable will be compelled to masturbate occasionally. Of course, the truth is that masturbation is quite healthy, whether you are alone or in a relationship. Besides the needed release it brings, it provides an opportunity for self-knowledge, and further, it can be a vehicle for finding the Goddess's physical presence in yourself.

The Goddess also exists in other women. Initially you can recognize Her in the women you relate to in non-sexual terms: your mother and grandmother, your sisters and friends, your teachers and co-workers, your daughters. Very many of us, whether or not we identify ourselves as lesbians, have taken a friendship with another woman a step further and become lovers. We were, in a large part, responding to the mirror of ourselves and of the Goddess in our friends. The conflicts that have developed because of these liaisons, especially since the Women's Movement began, are both sad and lately ironic. The natural attraction to another woman is often irresistible, yet we chide ourselves for it.

The essence of the matter is that you should always feel free to make love to the Goddess. If the Goddess is simply yourself, so be it. If you also find love for Her in another woman, this is appropriate whether or not you are exclusively woman-oriented.

Women who love only other women have committed themselves to the Goddess in another very special way. To some extent they exemplify the distinction between Christian pastorals and monastics. Both have dedicated themselves to a spiritual purpose, but monastics, like lesbians, are dedicated to a very concentrated focus on the deity. Women can always help other women find the Goddess, in the world and in themselves, but the woman who loves only women looks in a more single-minded way.

Women can help each other observe and commemorate the seasons of their female lives, the development of their bodies, menstruation, pregnancy and menopause. They can work together to relate the cycles of procreative energy to their artistic and imaginative lives.

As the Goddess is revered in the three phases of Her life, the Maiden, or youthful trust and innocence, the Mother, or nurturing, protecting woman, and Crone, or wise woman and teacher, women can, alone and between themselves, find these aspects in themselves. The role can take many forms: a woman expressing her Goddess as Mother may produce manuscripts or organized files for her food co-op instead of babies. And the roles may be intertwined, with the child knowing the Crone in herself and the elderly woman expressing the Maiden. Revering and recognizing all three in ourselves reclaims the value we once placed not only on these meanings in our own lives, but in the groups who most clearly represent them, children and the aged. (See Chapter 3 for more exploration of the Goddess's Maiden, Mother and Crone aspects.)

## . . . Men

Women who love men have a different opportunity for exploring the Goddess. First, there is the sacred feminine aspect in men themselves. "You are the Goddess" applies to men as well as women, trees, rocks and galaxies. It may be the single most repressed bit of knowledge and therefore one of the most important to recover and expose. If patriarchal society fears Her in women, they are terrified of Her in other men and, worst, in themselves. The woman Witch can learn more about men through finding the Goddess in them and exploring men's resistance to Her. A woman can learn more about the Goddess and the Goddess in herself by considering the role She takes in men's lives. And she can be a tool of virtual salvation for the man, Witch or not, as he seeks out the Goddess in himself. By seeking out the Goddess in himself, perhaps using this or similar books as opportunities to identify with women, a man will learn to empathize with women, to understand their reactions to restrictions and invasions of their power, and to find in himself those elements of nurturance and peacefulness which have been labeled "feminine" and therefore devalued by our society. Second, through love for and sexual union with a man, a woman reenacts the Goddess's love for her consort, the God, who is in most traditions also her brother and son.

The symbolism of the three aspects of the God take on a different role than the three aspects of the Goddess. Whereas in her Maiden, Mother, and Crone aspects, the Goddess stands primarily as an independent power, the Son, Lover, Brother God illustrates only His relationship to Her. This is emblematic of the Earth and the human race: She can stand without us, but we need Her. The Son reminds men of their inclusion in the Goddess, a necessary antidote in these times to destructive patriarchy, while the Lover and Brother permit men an equal relationship with Her and with the women in their lives. In the Lover, men are focused on women as desirable beings, an opportunity to merge with the Goddess. In the Brother, they are helpers and friends. Just as the Maiden, Mother and Crone exist both singly and together in a woman at different times in her life, so do the Son, Lover and Brother exist in a man, and will make themselves apparent to the woman relating to a man.

Sexuality is an integral part of the Sacred Year, the wheel of the seasons with its correspondences to the relationship of the Goddess and God. Different traditions assign different times for each occurrence, but basically the story is the same. The Goddess gives birth to Her Son, having carried the seed of the God in loneliness since His death. The seed is from Him, yet it is Him. (You can see here where the concept of the Trinity came from in Christianity.) When He grows to adulthood, They fall in love and consummate Their passion. Then He dies, in order that the Earth may thrive (the origin of Christ's death to save human souls), and the Goddess carries the seed until He is reborn. In actuality, the story is not so linear, as there must be parts for the Crone and the Brother as well. These are mysteries, and exist because of the difference between the simple circle of a year's seasons and the complexities of the much longer individual human life. In reenacting the divine relationship in your own life or in ritual, you may change the story to fit more closely the traditions or cultures with which you identify, or to include aspects of your own individual relationship(s).

I also want to encourage women to seek out the God in themselves. While it is more important initially for both women and men to identify the Goddess in themselves in order to counteract all the years of negation, there will come a time in each woman's life when identifying with the Son, the Lover and the Brother will offer knowledge otherwise hidden. This may be easier for women in lesbian relationships, first because people in relationships tend to instinctively fall into the divine relationship of Goddess and God, although this is not to say that one member of the relationship will always portray the Goddess and the other the God. Second, since a lesbian relationship provides such a concentrated attention to the Goddess, any anomalies may be discovered to be the aspects of the God. (Like the heterosexual woman, however, these women must be careful not to allow patriarchal notions of femininity and masculinity to mold them into polarized roles.) Next, the woman alone may find it increasingly possible to find both deities within herself. The woman relating to men may find it most difficult as there will be a tendency to polarize herself from the men in her life and miss the similarities between them and herself.

### Harm None and Do As You Will

Witchcraft is a religion recognizing personal responsibility. So where is the element of responsibility, of ethics in a Goddess-affirming view of sex?

The one basic law of most Witchcraft traditions, called the Rede, is stated as "so long as no harm comes to anyone or anything, do as you wish." Being so simply stated it would seem to imply Witchcraft's ethics might be straightforward and freedom might abound. No license for irresponsible behavior exists here, however. Each Witch must examine each situation and her own perception of it to understand fully what is least harmful. Interestingly, it seems the more laws that are written for conduct, the easier it is to find a loophole and squeeze out of responsibility. A directive no more convoluted than "harm none" sets one off on a quest for comprehensive benefit. It is important to note further that in Witchcraft the consequence of wrongdoing is a magnified return of the energy or intent of the action upon the actor. This is often termed "the threefold (or manifold) return of energy." It is not a case of "break a commandment and suffer everlasting torment." Each person examines her conduct and considers its effects upon her environment, including other people. Then for the sake of harming none, she considers the effect of the multiplied return of the energy to herself. No cosmic teller sits in judgment to dispense this energy. It is the nature of this energy to come back to the person, like the exchange of tides. It is the "response" in "responsibility."

In regard to sex there are different layers of responsibility. Clearly, we must avoid physical violence. Rape, for instance, is not only a dishonoring of the Mother in the harm inflicted on Her representative, a woman, but the physical, emotional and psychic harm is tremendous. Physical abuse of a woman or a child is no less damaging. Whereas there has been some tolerance for individual tastes in sadomasochistic sexual practice, the "consenting adults" assertion, it is important for both partners to seriously examine the roots of their willingness to hurt or be hurt and consider its implications on the well-being of their own spirit and the Goddess within. Sexual relationships with young people require introspection and consideration of the other's ability to consent. The immature are likely to be unable to make a sound judgment about their own or your sexual boundaries.

But what of the subtler ethics of sexuality? Initially, there is the need for recognition of individual expression, the need to allow others to follow their own spiritual and Earthly paths. No one can decide, based on her own judgment, which paths are the correct ones. To block another's path is to harm her, to prevent her from reaching whatever destination she is meant for in this or any of her lives. Of course, this also goes for one's own expression. Each of us has a responsibility to follow her own path directed by her individual intuition, not the commands or judgments of her family, friends, social, political or spiritual leaders or movements, or society.

A very difficult question to face when seeking one's fullest sexual expression is "Who is speaking?" That is, is the individual following her own path or following guidelines set by others? Is she, for instance, making love because she and her partner want to, or is she submitting to the other's pressure, or fear of seeming inhibited or failing to meet the other's needs? Is a woman in a relationship with a man because it is the true expression of her sexuality in this lifetime or because it is "normal" to be heterosexual, because Mom and Dad would approve, because others in her coven don't accept lesbian relationships?

In *The Medicine Woman's Inner Guidebook*, Carol Bridges brings up the concept of mixing energies, or auras, with a person or persons with whom one has intimate relations. She encourages the seeker to ask, "Do I give the gift of my sexuality to one I would like to become?"[1] In sexual union we share a part of ourselves, take on a part of our partner's wholeness. If one has chosen a partner for irresponsible reasons, perhaps a partner who disregards her interests, or a partner who is willing to be manipulated by her, the exchange of energies is unwilling and damaged.

Patriarchal philosophies, so interested in controlling our bodies and preventing us from making decisions about pro-creation, have labored long to deny us information about and access to contraception. At the very least, the providers of contraceptive devices have been irresponsible and callous about creating safe methods and providing complete informa-tion and education in regard to them. It is part of self-empowerment for a woman to make an informed decision about whether or not to have a baby. Further, it is essential to her own health to have the necessary information to choose the safest contraceptive method.

In this era of the monster AIDS we are increasingly aware of the dangers of ignorance. In the case of sexually transmitted diseases in general, this ignorance is fostered by patriarchal institutions' unwillingness and even opposition to providing full, balanced, objective and accessible information on the nature, spread and prevention of the disease. It is also involved in the refusal by many men to use condoms, which might help control the contagion, because they are unwilling to be re-sponsible. That ignorance is explicit in the continued super-stitious prohibition of prostitution, which results in poor health care and poor living conditions for the women illegally involved. On a broader scale, the ignorance about AIDS spe-cifically and the encouragement of homophobic paranoia by Fundamentalists is expressed through hysterical reactionism and a return to repressive anti-gay laws. To "harm none" we as a society must encourage education about venereal disease and its prevention, a sense of mutual responsibility by sexual part-ners, and devote more of our funds and attention to finding cures. As individuals we must take on the responsibility our-selves to be well-informed and conscious of preventive measures and to treat others with the respect they deserve without the paranoia that often cripples us.

Finally, what of the subtlest of sexual injuries, the ones stemming from personal rejection? Each of us has the right and the responsibility to decline any activity that we feel is not right for us. Yet rejection goes much deeper, to the persistent belittling or lack of concern for an individual because of some real or imagined trait, or of whole groups for not fitting some accepted standard. As women, we know the damage which is done by the patent rejection of those assumed to be weaker, whether physically or intellectually. We are in a position, therefore, to assess the harm we ourselves do to women of color, women of different sexual and affectional identification, disabled women, fat women, older women, or, for that matter, men, by failing to view each individual for her or his unique characteristics. Because of the tension widely associated with sex in our culture, it would be wise to consider how pressures as divers as clothing styles and representations of the Goddess in art affect our or others' sense of the Goddess in our own bodies.

*Our spiritual heritage* is rich and the widening rebirth of the religion of the Great Goddess is replete with talented and resourceful people, exploring, recreating, offering what they are learning, thinking, crafting to those who might come after. Recognition of the role of sexuality, whether as affirmation of the needs and pleasures of our own bodies or as a seat of energy to be molded for magickal transformation, can come from the reclamation of the Goddess through understanding of ancient herstory, and through an understanding of how the Goddess and her gift of bodily pleasure and creativity has been twisted through the power struggle with patrifocal religions and civilizations. By reaffirming the feminine divine in ourselves and fostering its rebirth in men, and taking the responsibility to care for each other as we would prefer to be cared for, we can help our Mother Earth survive the conflict as we tear ourselves away from the Piscean Age and greet the liberation of the Aquarian. However, before we can even begin to affirm the Goddess in the world and especially in other women and men, we must love Her in our own bodies.

[1] Bridges, Carol, *The Medicine Woman's Inner Guidebook*, Self-published, 1981, p. 22.

# 2

## *Sex Magick for Women*

The accumulation of mixed signals contemporary women have received has resulted in sexual confusion for most of us. With so many different voices and messages about correct, healthy, acceptable behavior, we encounter doubt or guilt at many turns. We receive tremendous pressure from our culture to shape our bodies, our personalities, our clothing and even our faces to meet an artificial definition of sexual desirability. Where freedom and joy should reside, we find struggle: struggle within ourselves, within relationships and within our communities.

Even those of us who have overcome social strictures against unauthorized non-marital and/or same gender relationships find deep layers of blocked self-determination. Thanks to messages about psychologically healthy boundaries we are nagged by worries about the quantity, nature and quality of sexual expression. Do I do this or that too much or too little or with the right type or number of partners? Is it all right for me to initiate or to follow another's lead? What will so-and-so think of me if I want to do this or that? Am I conforming to cultural standards of weight, height, coloring, and, if not, how do I do so?

Going deeper than the issue of sexual practice itself, we find ourselves in a dubious and often estranged relationship with our own bodies. The message in childhood was that we should not be selfish or greedy. Before being applied to sex and other aspects of adult relationships, greed was applied to the desire for food and material possessions. We were told to eat less, no matter how little or how much we ate. Even if we were encouraged at home to bedeck ourselves, the motive was to teach us to conform, to keep within the bounds of "fashion," and even then the criticism sometimes came that we were frivolous, vain, shallow. If we were not, then we were ridiculed for nonconformity.

After puberty we battled with the inner conflict of our own desire to experiment with sex, with the admonitions from parents, church and popular psychology not to masturbate or be "loose," with manipulation from boys to have sex or with rejection because we were undesirable. We arrived at adulthood stunted in our personalities and in our sexual identity by all the conflicting commands and judgments.

Recognition of the Goddess within and magickal practice can begin to strip away the bonds of self-denial and confusion. It can neutralize the voices. It can shed light and understanding on the mixed messages. It can return the natural experience and expression of pleasure and joy that comes from self-determination and unbound opportunity. Further, releasing the feminine divine within us can empower our magickal self, enabling each of us to energize our rituals, meditations, and magickal workings, and make them more effective. The first step is to walk out of the other-defined woman, look into the mirror, and see Her within you.

## You Are the Goddess

Patriarchal religions often speak of the presence of God in everything and specifically in the human heart. In reality they have separated the divine from the human. There is, after all, a difference between the divine being present in all the world and being the world itself, otherwise dominion over the Earth would be a contradiction. Adherents are urged to surrender themselves to God. Recently I considered joining a group for adult children of alcoholics, but reneged when I learned of their use of the Alcoholics Anonymous 12 Steps, which include an affirmation of one's powerlessness and a surrender of one's problems to God. When a friend tried to reassure me that these days the groups usually replace the word "God" with "Higher Power," I had to explain that the change of terminology would not suffice. We ARE the Goddess and share Her power in our own lives. A Witch does not "surrender" herself or release her own power to any higher authority but rather works with the Goddess to empower herself and other women.

You are the Goddess. Each person, female or male, and each and every living or non-living thing in the universe is the Goddess. The mystery, if it be one, is that She is all things and yet She is each thing individually. In ancient times people divided the Goddess into thousands of Goddesses. Every tree, every rock, every animal had its own deity. Each had its own personality and powers. Some Witches today continue the naming of thousands of Goddesses and Gods, others name only one Goddess but respect the individual spirit of people, rocks, trees and so forth. The more "scientifically" inclined point to the common bases of matter and energy and call the sum "Goddess" and each of us localizations of these. However you look at it, you are inseparable from the Goddess. You can no more revere Her and serve Her without revering and serving yourself than a cat can give birth to puppies.

On a simple, very straightforward basis, this means that the Goddess experiences everything each of us experiences. She feels the flow of streams, the erosion of the rock it flows over, the texture of algae in a fish's mouth, the terror of a mouse caught by an owl, the heat of the Earth's core, the loneliness of a star in distant space, the tearing apart of the atom in a nuclear explosion, the earthworm's patient progress through a compost pile and the pain of rejection when a disabled child is taunted. And She feels your sorrows and pleasures, your first gasp of air, your first true friendship, the horror at an "F" on your report card, your first kiss, your regret as you lose some of the magic of childhood, your labor pains, your grief, your reflective satisfaction over a life well-lived, your death, and then all over again in a different body. Each twinge of despair or satisfaction is part of Her vitality, the cycles of Her immortality. In return She offers you the power of transformation, of insight, of intuition, of direct communication with Her.

She deserves the best you can give Her, and that is the best you can give yourself. By denying yourself something you need or want, by allowing patriarchal strictures to fill you with guilt, by sacrificing yourself needlessly, you are denying Her, sacrificing Her, filling Her with guilt and the dominance of patriarchy. Certain followers of the God Krishna believe that He experiences human life vicariously through us, and therefore seek perfection in physical pleasure. The Goddess, being wholly present and not at all vicarious, is even more truly due this kindness. You need not feel guilty about Her/your past sufferings, nor strive to avoid all future sorrows or pitfalls, for She understands the battle you are waging and the problems of human life. But you can seek to free yourself of the chains male domination have placed on Her/you. You can begin to love yourself and Her in you.

When you look into the mirror, what do you say to yourself? "My breasts are too small" . . . "I'm ugly" . . . "I have a big ass" . . . "My hair is too stringy." When you see those or other "undesirable" features in another woman, do you think the same thoughts? The likelihood is yes, even if for only a second. We are notoriously critical of each other. Do you draw your Goddess images in the image of some thin model? If the Goddess came into the room today, and she had a big nose, a scrawny neck, was in a wheelchair, or weighed about 350 pounds, would you be disappointed? Undoubtedly. That's what you've been trained to be. This is the misogyny of self-repugnance.

Every time you look into the mirror you are looking at the Goddess. Every time you wince at your midriff bulge, you are seeing a defect in Her. Learning to love Her entails learning to see yourself as beautiful. This, by the way, goes for your emotions and personality as well. Anger is Her fury, dissatisfaction and complaining are Her cathartic wails, laziness is Her luxuriant indolence. Is there a line to be drawn? Again, as stated in the earlier chapter on Wiccean ethics, that question bears two new ones[1]. Can you divorce truth from programming? And would you want to receive the energy sent out returned to you magnified? Every time you say or think the words "I should" or "I shouldn't" you should stop and ask those questions. For instance, "I should get to work and stop being so lazy." Are you giving in to the Puritan Work Ethic, which contends that work for its own sake is superior to relaxation for its own sake? Are you afraid of failing in the eyes of your mother, your boss, your lover or your children? Are you simply distracting yourself from that repose which might allow you to be reflective, or perhaps simply denying your body (and the Goddess) some rest and pleasure and fun? Or is your "laziness" a trick you've invented to avoid self-fulfillment? Are you allowing things to pile up around you to furnish evidence for your conviction that you are a bad and undeserving person? Are you hiding from yourself and success? In essence, what is it you (or more likely your society's strictures) call "laziness?" Once you have made up your mind on that one, ask what energy is going out and whether you'd want it. Will your ability to relax occasionally without self-reproach make you a more cheerful and self-actualized woman? Will you spend this reflective time building your own power? Will the calmness you gain spill over onto friends and family? Or will the procrastination rob you of satisfaction? Will it teach your children that you cannot be counted on to spend time with them? Will disorganization wind up more of a burden than resisting the Work Ethic would?

Another valuable example is the drive for fitness and a slender shape, or self-reproach for being a "beanpole" and flat-chested. When you say "I should lose weight" or "I should look more voluptuous," is that really you talking? Is it, perhaps, really your father, the women you work with, your lover, a man who insults you on the street, the doctors, drug companies, spa owners, and women's magazine editors who make a fortune off convincing you that you're ugly or unfit? If you join an exercise class or go on that diet, what energy will come back? Will you, in fact, feel better physically? Will you be sought after and desired more than you are now? Will you be happier? Or will you go on guilt binges where you gorge with junk food and feel ill instead of eating to satisfaction the wealth of healthful and well-balanced food? Will you fail and justify your self-hate further? Will you succeed and become self-righteously reproachful of others' "failures?" Will you deny your own natural shape and permit fashion to rule you? Will you perpetuate the myth of a uniform, impersonal ideal?

If you can begin to recognize the Goddess in yourself, you are a giant step closer to being empowered. You will know your own needs and desires and will be better able to interact with the world around you.

Meditation is always a valuable tool for self-transformation. In a relaxed state you are better able to contact your deep psyche, to explore previously hidden or obscured meanings and to implant suggestions for growth on any particular area of concern, including body image. The relaxation itself has beneficial physical and psychic effects, lowering stress and energizing the spirit. Using guided imagery, a "story" in which you imagine yourself taking part and noting how you perceive surroundings, people, situations, meeting and conversing with guides and the Goddess Herself and obtaining gifts that reveal understanding, can be an active tool for getting at difficult issues. If you feel you are too fat, you might take yourself into guided imagery where you discuss your feelings with a spirit guide, ask questions about what fatness means to you, meet fat Goddesses who revel in their size, and begin to teach yourself, while in the receptive meditative state, to love your body as it is. If you are very nervous about sex, but don't know why, you can likewise explore your feelings by making love to your partner or others within your meditation, to provide positive experiences to help heal your nervousness.

The following are examples of meditations you may use specifically to identify physically with the Goddess, to come to understand that you *are* She, that you cannot truthfully objectify Her or yourself. Whenever you meditate, it is important to remember to always ground and center yourself. These techniques are important so that you will not "space out," feel disoriented after the meditation or experience your meditation as insubstantial and hard to recall. Through grounding you anchor yourself, providing yourself with a sense of security and connection to the Earth, and free yourself from the distractions of your day. For Goddess worshipers, grounding and centering also reaffirms the bond with Her as Earth Mother. You do this by relaxing through deep breathing, through tightening and releasing muscles systematically, beginning with your toes and working up, and then picturing yourself as a tree firmly rooted in the Earth, or you may choose to imagine a stout cord attached to the base of your spine and to the core of the Earth. Look through the meditations in the pages of this and other books until you find a method that speaks to you. Centering techniques involve creating sacred space in your deep mind, building an imaginary bridge over a creek, clearing away brush from a campsite, concentrating on your spine as a firm but elastic channel of energy, or floating freely in water or air. Also, whenever you come out of a meditation, do it slowly and find your personal way of coming out thoroughly, stimulate your senses with food or scents, place your hands palms down on the ground to feel reconnected, and whirl or jump to invigorate and reorient yourself.

## Meditations For Identifying With the Goddess

(Both meditations are suitable either as a solitary exercise or in a group. In the first, while each person will identify with the Earth, you may see the others as sister planets. In the second, the other meditators may be different aspects of the Goddess. In fact, you might want to select individual favorite Goddesses, discuss their attributes, and visualize those attributes in each woman during the meditation.)

### Meditation 1

Relax. Center. Ground yourself. Breath deeply and rhythmically. Begin to feel each breath as the ebb and flow of waves on a beach. Slowly begin to sway with the rhythm. You are the Earth. You can feel your almost imperceptible rotation. You can sense the chill on your night side, and the radiance of the sun on your day side. The top of your head and the bottom of your feet are faintly cold. Great oceans move with your breath. Great rivers cross your land and feed you. You can look out at your own moon, which silently circles you and your sister planets on their own paths. Far away other suns are circled by other planets. You feel the pull of each and in turn pull mildly upon them. If you wish, begin to hum a tone or a succession of tones as you feel the different cycles touch you in turn. Be aware of your Earth body: sense the valleys and mountains, the forests and deserts, the creatures scattered throughout. Feel deep inside your molten core. Feel the change in your tilt and the change it effects on your surface. Stay with these images as long as you like. Come out slowly.

## Meditation 2

Prepare your environment. However you imagine the Goddess, place yourself in the surroundings that you imagine for the Goddess. For instance, prepare yourself a "throne," a chair covered with draped fabric and set candles and incense all around. Go into the woods. Or simply develop a mental image of a temple or mountaintop that you can keep with you during the meditation. Relax. Center. Ground yourself. Begin to breathe deeply: inhale through your nose in quick, full breaths. Exhale through your mouth, just as sharply. Feel that with each intake of air you are drawing in the energy, the movement, the sounds, the thoughts and prayers of the whole world, the whole universe. As you exhale, you return to it nourishment, both physical and spiritual. Now, look (with open eyes or your mind's eye) on your surroundings. You are the Goddess in Her temple. Open Your arms in a grand gesture and smile on all things. Speak or think a blessing on each, promising it Your love and granting it continuing energy. Hear the wind and sea and rain mingle with the chants of people all over the world. They are singing to You. Send them Your blessings, too. Remember when You created the universe and the planet You gaze on now. Remember the many, many renewals of seasons, the Earth's and Your own. Remember a favorite story or myth, in the first person, as you recall the events through the Goddess's eyes. Bring yourself out of the meditation slowly.

*Both of these* meditations are likely to raise a great deal of energy. Help it dissipate naturally through vigorous movement: dance, spin, sing and clap, or hug everything in sight. Ground whatever energy remains by focusing it through your hands pressed together and pointed downward into the Earth. This will keep you from "overcharging" and feeling scattered or out of touch.

## Loving Your Body

The physical hurdle is the main block to a deeper identification with the Goddess. After all, our culture has bequeathed to us a belief that we are essentially only bodies that must conform to male standards and be ever at men's disposal. Through the exercise below and similar exercises you can begin to loosen the hold that belief has on you. No matter how empowered you may feel in ritual, the moment you flinch at your reflection or indulge in exaggerated guilt at that extra cookie, you have negated your liberation in the Goddess. This hurdle overcome, you may begin to examine your identity as the Goddess in your relationships, in your daily activities, in your creative expression, in ritual or meditation, and in sex.

Once you have recognized the origin of your self-repugnance as patriarchal demands imposed on you, your next step will be to find new ways of looking at yourself. Try these exercises.

## Exercise 1

This one sounds easy, but it isn't. Go to your mirror. Stand close and stare into the eyes of the woman reflected there. Keep staring. Most people will sooner or later blush and look away. Don't feel sad: you are, in essence, looking at a stranger. Repeat the exercise until you find yourself getting to know this woman, yourself. Repeat it until you smile a warm welcome into her eyes.

## Exercise 2

Go to the mirror again and look at yourself. Now go to the books on your shelf, your back issues of feminist spiritual magazines or to the library. Find pictures of Goddesses. There will be photographs of prehistoric sculpture, drawings or photographs of Ancient Greek or Roman statues and paintings and copies of ancient Hindu and other religious art. Since many early Christian female saints were based on pagan deities, you might look for early medieval representations of them. Notice your first impressions of these images and notice possibly your vestigial self-disgust. Is the woman pictured diverging from your culture's ideal for sexual attractiveness? Is she, perhaps, thick of thigh, fat, the "wrong" skin color, too tall, too short, too masculine? Now begin to recognize in your mind and spirit that these are other peoples' representations of the Goddess. They are the ideal of their cultures, the representation of all that is bountiful, loving and beautiful. In your own way, venerate and admire these images. Worship the Goddess. Speak to the Goddess in each drawing or photograph, telling Her what you are feeling, what you are beginning to recognize as beautiful in Her images. Make a composite, several composites, in your mind of the elements in each to which you are drawn.

Now, go back to the mirror. Look at yourself thoroughly, lovingly, and recognize those features that you have seen in images of the Goddess. Smile as you press down or puff up, exaggerating this feature and that, and gently caress each one. Pay special attention to those features you formerly disliked.

## Exercise 3

Once you feel successful with Exercises 1 and 2 in this chapter, try out the effects in the following ways. Go to your closet. Decide which clothes perpetuated your old image of yourself. When you buy or make new clothes, replace those old ones with the sort of clothing you think the Goddess would want to wear if she were to take human form today. When you go out into the world, look at women who don't fit the stereotype of modern feminine beauty. Look for pudgy teenagers, athletically-built women, women of other races and national origins than your own, older women, tall women, disabled women, women of all shapes, sizes, ages, colors, economic backgrounds. Remember the Goddess pictures and smile at the Goddess in each woman you see. Each and every woman is an animate statue of the Goddess.

*Early in the current* Women's Movement there was a good deal written about women's inner conflicts about their own genitals. We have fretted over breast size and shape for a very long time, falling prey to brassiere manufacturers' promises to "correct" any "flaws" nature gave us. This may seem akin to men's anxieties about penis size, except that penises are not subject to changing fashions. The couturiers don't stress large penises one year and small ones ten years later, as has been the case with women's breasts. A similar change has occurred for hip size. Every woman has heard the old standard of feminine "vital statistics:" 36–22–36. About 20 years ago I read where *Playboy Magazine* had altered this to 34–24–35. Certainly ready-made clothing bears out the shift to less ample features, since women with more than the required differences between breast, waist and hips find it difficult to buy whole outfits in a single size.

In greater contrast to men's and women's views of their own bodies is our attitude toward our external reproductive organs. Male genitals are a source of pride, the "family jewels." Women don't share this pride. In fact, we are rather disgusted by our vulvas and vaginas. We spend millions of dollars per year to clean and deodorize them, and have been told by manufacturers of the light sanitary napkin that we need to protect our clothing from our vulvas and vaginas all month long, not just during our menstrual flow. The menstrual flow itself is "the curse," a time when we redouble our efforts to make ourselves as pristeen and thoroughly inoffensive as possible, live in horror of being seen with bloodstains on our clothes and wouldn't even think of having sex. Many of us share anxieties about receiving cunnilingus for fear of offending our partners, and it is a rare woman who has spent time examining and even admiring her genitals.

Some of this self-repugnance comes from general insecurity about our bodies, some from a specific fear of smelling bad. But much of it is undoubtedly based on a feeling that lacking a penis, we are incomplete. Anti-feminists are only too willing to capitalize on Freud's comments on penis envy. The taunts thrown at feminists that we are castrators, that all we really want is to be able to pee standing up flew even thicker and faster during the early 1970s. Radical feminists have attacked this problem from the very start. Tee Corinne's drawings, including those published in her *Labiaflowers*, and Betty Dodson's *Self Love and Orgasm* (see Bibliography) were some of the early efforts to bring female sexuality in its most intimate and personal aspects to the attention of reawakening female consciousness. They presented us with the vulva and vagina as objects to explore, to admire, providing us with examples of the diversity of color and shapes, and portraying them as flowers.

Witches have a unique opportunity to learn to love our own genitals as we have a greater wealth of artwork and articles on genital imagery in our magazines and books, and because we recognize that each of us is the Goddess. Feminist artists frequently represent the Goddess with vaginal imagery of the sea pouring forth, or forests being born, from the Earth's own vagina. (More awareness of genital symbolism among most Witches will be explored in Chapter 3.)

## Exercise 4

A simple exercise for awakening appreciation of one's genitals follows along the line of the one for body image. Instead of Goddess images in general, find drawings of Goddesses which include or concentrate on vaginal symbolism. There is a plenitude of such art in feminist spiritual publications such as *Womanspirit Magazine* or *Sagewoman* and in the work of artist Prairie Jackson. If you cannot locate a copy of Corinne's *Labiaflowers*, take a leaf from her book and gather various types of flowers or pictures of them. Use a magnifying hand mirror and a good light source and begin to examine your own genitals. Notice the similarities in shape to the drawings, and notice your own individual uniqueness. Admire the color, texture, arrangement of your pubic hair and labia. Smell and taste your fingertips to get a sense of your own perfumes. In Dodson's Liberating Masturbation workshops, women used plastic speculums, available from women's health centers, to see further into their vaginas and to take photographs or make drawings of each other's unique beauty.

*If you find yourself* aroused, don't be alarmed or ashamed. The next step after learning to love your body is making love to your body. Masturbation has a very bad name in our culture. While it has progressed from much of the irrational fear that was once promulgated, that masturbating would cause blindness or hairy palms, or the brutality once practiced to prevent it (clitorectomies to rob girls of the satisfactions of sex, particularly masturbation, were not uncommon in Victorian times), masturbation is still a taboo subject. Kinsey found that more heterosexual men and women would admit to homosexual experiences than would admit to masturbating. Autosexuality carries connotations of selfishness, of interpersonal inadequacy, of obsessive sexuality and of perversion. Sex manuals have come to the point of sanctioning and even encouraging its practice, especially as part of love-making between two people. Yet our fears persist. A person may become furious or upset if she finds or learns that her partner still masturbates. It is either a selfish act on the partner's part, or evidence that she is not being fulfilled by the lover. I remember as a teenager on a two-week vacation in Ireland, vowing not to masturbate while there so as not to sully that special, magickal place. That was ironic, since had I been a Witch then I would have realized that masturbation would have honored the place, being a valuable tool for magick.

You are the Goddess. Whenever you make love to yourself you are making love to the Goddess. The intense physical awareness of masturbating gives you an opportunity to explore your body and to enhance your Goddess-awareness. It is a wonderful relaxing and centering tool, and can precede meditation. Since it can be more spontaneous and impulsive than sex with a partner, it can be used to heighten the spiritual energy of ritual. Make love to yourself before ritual to relax and center, use masturbation as an energy-raising tool during ritual, or frame the entire ritual around it. It need not be a public act where others could be made uncomfortable; you can easily confine your activities to solitary ritual or ritual with a partner, or use hidden devices, like ben wa balls or your own creative imagination to incorporate masturbation into your more public rituals.

### Masturbation Ritual

Prepare your altar. Decorate it with items having particular sexual symbolism to you, perhaps an iris, a half of a melon, a seashell or an erotic depiction of the Goddess. Burn a musky incense and light a single pink, red, or violet candle. Be sure to speak to each item, lovingly and gratefully. You may be sky-clad (nude) or loosely robed. Have flavored love oils handy. (These can be purchased or made using natural vegetable oils and fruit syrups. Don't use raw fruit or vegetables inside your vagina, as they have natural bacteria that can cause unpleasant reactions.) Create your circle by passing an athame or medicine rattle from the east to south to west to north and around to east again, invoking the spirit of each direction. (These are east, the direction associated with air, south with fire, west with water, and north with Earth. See Chapter 3 for broader associations.) Make the circle large enough so that you can lie down in it. Invoke the Goddess. Tell Her what you are doing, that you will be making love to yourself and Her. Relax, center, and ground yourself. Breathe deeply and rhythmically, and begin to lovingly caress your body. Identify each part of your body with a feature of the Earth: mountains, valleys, forests, rivers, ocean, core. Simultaneously, concentrate on the woman you are making love to. She is the Goddess. Touch Her as you would a partner or as you would wish to be touched. Use the sexual energy you build up to create psychic energy around you, drawing from the sun or the moon or a crystal to replenish yourself, until the final burst and then denouement of energy at orgasm(s). That energy will remain afterwards, available for any magick work you want to do. When you are finished with your work, thank the Goddess, and open your circle by reversing the direction of your athame and greeting and thanking each direction from north to west to south to east. Give yourself a hug.

## Sharing the Goddess Within

So many of us who have been involved with women's spirituality have found more than just a comfortable niche for our ideas, our creative expression, our relationships. We have truly "found" the Goddess, that divinity both within and without ourselves that has spoken to us from childhood and speaks to us still. Enculturated to turn our love outside of ourselves, to other people, to the community, to God, we now can focus that love on ourselves. This is as true for expressions of our sexuality as any other mode of loving; in fact, we can learn and have been learning to affirm our sexuality through and FOR the Goddess, loving ourselves and Her through ourselves, and turning that long-repressed energy into magickal power for transformation of ourselves and our planet.

Still, attending to our own divinity has never meant disregarding others. On the contrary, like ants, gorillas, penguins, and cats and dogs, we are social animals. We love to share, we love to nurture and provide care and resources for others. Witness the proliferation of Goddess culture in recent years, how the movement reached out to you, and how you long to reach out to it. Recognizing and loving the Goddess within you, you will automatically share Her. You will shine with Her energy, and that positive energy will overflow and be gratefully, if unknowingly, accepted by your loved ones, acquaintances, and strangers.

You can more actively share Her by explaining your glow. With friends who are open to your spirituality, you can offer the ideas and exercises in this chapter. They need not be confined to your woman friends, as men can adapt them to their own use, using different symbols, more phallic in nature, or intentionally empathizing with women by becoming one in fantasy. Partners of either gender may want to go through the exercises with you, observing your physical identification with the Goddess. Further suggestions can be found later in this book, including how you might pass on what you have learned to your children.

As you share with the others in your life, you will find that the return of your loving energy will feed you, will foster further recognition of the Goddess within. It will heighten your positive relationships, which will become more fertile and heighten your self-empowerment. The psychic energy you will raise will be available for channeling into ritual practice, into magick.

---

[1] Wicce refers to a female practitioner of magick. See Laurie Cabot, *The Power of the Witch*, New York, New York: Delta Books, 1989, p. 14.

# 3

# Sex in Ritual: Sexual Magick

Patriarchal religions, while decrying secular humanism for its elevation of humans in the place of God, have conversely insisted on separating the human being from the animal that she is. In biological classification we are primates which are mammals which are vertebrates, all included in the general classification of animals. As one result of raising ourselves above animals, we often use their names, for instance "snakes," "worms," "cats," "pigs," to insult each other. We respond to a violent act by disclaiming, "He behaved like an animal!" Certain sexual positions, such as "doggie-style," or intercourse from behind in a kneeling position, are viewed by some as too blatantly sexual. All these aspersions ignore the fact that we ARE animals. Further, they imply a position between the rest of nature and God. Since God, in patrifocal religion, is self-contained and asexual, then humans must strive to be the same to attain His favor.

As animals, however, reproduction, whether through cellular division or mating, is a primal urge. Seen from a non-homocentric viewpoint, the ultimate purpose of biology, of life, is to sustain and reproduce itself. That vital impulse, to survive and to bear young, is part of not only being animals, but of being ANIMATE. In some organisms, the parent does not even survive the act of procreating, the instinct of self-preservation being subjugated to the instinct to bear fruit. For example, salmon die after spawning, some insects kill their mates once pregnant or die themselves once they lay their eggs. Annual plants drop their seed and then wither. Sex is the vital, the most central urge of the living thing, whether or not it is the sole urge. As animals, we are no exception.

As Witches, we venerate the Earth and the symbol of its combined energies as a deity, as the Goddess or the marriage of the Goddess and God. It is She who has placed these primal impulses into every living being, into us. Sex is therefore the primal spark of life in us, as we are in a class of animals that mates.

This piece of information goes contrary to so many of our homocentric notions that most of us will automatically reject this very simple concept. It seems to imply that we, as humans, are perpetually erotic, even lewd beings. The implications of this bias are complex and misleading. It describes sex as a less significant and shameful urge, rather than identifying its positive and creative nature. It focuses on reproduction of children only. Even other animals channel this sexual energy into other aspects of their lives. They go about the business of surviving, creating, bonding with mates and communities of their kind. As humans we channel our sexual energy into our own more elaborate versions of all these and further into intellectual, emotional, spiritual and artistic endeavors. We use the spark of life, the generative urge, for more than the creation of progeny, for the creation of great beauty, whether fashioned from the material or from the joy of love of partner, family, or community, and, like many other animals, we are not limited to heterosexual practice or love.

When we distance ourselves from the denial of the primal sexual energy which grants so much power to the creations of our lives, the denial so important to patrifocal religion, and instead identify with it and with its involvement in the universal creative urge, we validate it. We free it in ourselves, empower it, and in return receive its power. It can become a tool for spiritual empowerment.

As humans, we are creatures highly attuned to symbolism. Our dreams reach past recreation of daily activities to complex, often puzzling and meaningful images. Our unique use of language is the epitome of our aptitude and intuition for the use of symbols. Each word, each framing of them in complete concepts, is a symbol of concrete or abstract ideas. We go further to the artistic use of symbols in song, graphic art, poetry, the rich embroidery of fiction. We imbue our relationships with other humans and the natural or human-made environment with symbols of kinship, of belonging, of personal identity.

Ritual is the creation of symbolic activities and surroundings to induce a frame of mind, a certain level of perception. Something as simple as marking the beginning of the work day by flipping the page of a desk calendar is a ritual: done on a regular basis, it alters the mind, defines the purpose of ensuing activity. Busy families sometimes insist on a Sunday meal together as a symbol, a reminder of their unity. Whether or not the deeper meaning of a symbol is recognized consciously, ritual is the conscious act of arranging symbols. Religious practice actively uses ritual to prepare a physical, emotional and mental space for communion with the deity. As Witches, we use rituals which are traditional to certain paths, rituals suggested by experienced ritual-makers. We draw from these to recognize commonly accepted symbols or improvise on the basis of intuitive recognition of individual or shared meaning.

Primal urges, such as the urge for sex, express themselves whether or not we are conscious of them. In these days of greater understanding of human psychology, we are only too aware of how highly repressed urges can erupt into unexpected sickness, pain or violence, whether inflicted on ourselves or on those around us. The power behind the urge for sex is apparent to those who would seek to hold it down as well as to those who recognize its ability to give joy and love. This is a power that may, once its creative and sacred natures are affirmed, lend its energy to any number of pursuits: artistic, practical, bonding, the psychic and spiritual.

In this chapter we will explore how this power can be found, fostered and expressed in magickal practice. The first step for the seeker is to discover it within herself, through the recognition and affirmation of the Goddess within. Identifying with Her, the seeker will find the Goddess's generative energy within herself and discover how it expresses itself in her as pure physical pleasure or creativity. There are a number of tools available to the Witch to help to direct this power toward celebration of the Goddess and the practice of magick.

The simple act of celebration, the creation and enactment of ritual is the most basic of these tools. No matter what tradition you follow, no matter what other tools and symbols one uses, concentration on the Goddess and on communion with Her is the foundation of all sex magick in practice. Whether one does no more than light a candle and state an affirmation or engages in a formalized ritual in a large circle, the power of sex, of love, is there and can be harnessed.

Many of our meditations and rituals begin with relaxation and exercises for grounding and centering. These generally involve visualizing some attachment to the Earth through the base of one's spine, the location of the Root Chakra (energy center) and of one's basic physical instincts. The energy one draws from the Earth through this and other lower body chakras, including the center of sexual energy, becomes the vibration that influences the power of the remainder of the chakras. Equally, when one draws cosmic light to empower one's meditation or ritual, energy fills the lower body chakras as well as the higher. Thus deeply physical, even visceral, energy imbues and enables any power one raises.

Sensing and attending to such power tends to snowball its effects. Like an automobile's electrical system which sparks the piston's rise and fall to turn the wheels which in turn charge the battery, the sense of empowerment feeds itself when consciously identified with the Goddess within. A third source of energy is advisable, much like the car's gasoline, so most power raising or spell rituals instruct the practitioner to draw energy from another source as well as from within. This power may be the moon or sun, a charged crystal or some other strong source. The buildup of this energy is palpable, and there is no mistaking when one has accomplished it. Awareness further aids the ritualist by enabling her not only to build but to direct the power to some vessel of need, whether a specific object or person or to the world in general. Invoking the automobile image again, it is both ineffective and unwise to "gun one's motor," simply to keep the power within. Send the raised energy outside of yourself, whether to make it available to someone in need of it, or to the Goddess who will return it to you as self-transformation.

## Sexual Symbols in Ritual

Sexual symbolism can be found in many aspects of effective ritual, including the form of the ritual itself, relationships within the circle or coven and in the tools found on a Goddess altar.

## Form

Ritualists know that certain psychic or material tools and their symbolism are useful keys to raising deeply rooted energy for use in practical magick. The form of the ritual itself provides both continuity and concentration. It fosters an environment, a state of mind that is receptive to the Goddess and to communion with Her. It provides a method for drawing energy from the Earth and the cosmos which activates our own energy centers, including the sexual. Ritual shares with the act of lovemaking a basic form, of initiation and development, of building energy, of climax and denouement. Is it any wonder, then, that many Witches find through physical as well as emotional signs that they have been sexually aroused? Just as in lovemaking, the parts that you will emphasize in ritual will vary and will depend on the moods and needs of the participants at the given time. As a result, to be too rigid and dogmatic about the form of ritual, to adhere slavishly to accepted rites, can hamper both the experience of the ritual and the magickal work. A skillful ritual-crafter will be sensitive to the moods of her circle just as a good lover is to the needs of her partner.

A good deal has been made in recent years of the differences between female and male orgasm, noting the cyclic nature of a woman's sexual response and her ability to orgasm soon, even immediately, after coming. Men, it is said, have a more linear pattern, building directly to climax, then needing to rest some time before engaging again in lovemaking. Needless to say, for every "rule" there are plenty who will offer exceptions, there being women who experience linear arousal and men who can orgasm many times. Each Witch who considers the sexual symbolism of form in a ritual should explore her own experience and intuition to draw up a ritual which speak to her and the others for whom she is performing it. It might be interesting and revealing to create "linear" rituals to help celebrants experience the God, and "cyclic" (repeating sections, having a build up to magickal work more than once in a long celebration) for those identifying with the Goddess. Then listen to

how your circle or coven reacts and how effective the identification was for them.

## Relationships

Some Witchcraft traditions have always recognized and affirmed the place of sexuality in ritual. While the outcries of
detractors that we engage in ritual orgies appears to be greatly
exaggerated, the element of sexuality is represented through
the relationships within a circle and through use of ritual form
and symbols to build available energy. Some traditions limit
the teacher-student relationship within a group to different
gender pairs, the woman teaching the man, who then teaches a
woman. For traditions that venerate the bond between the
Goddess and the God, the pairing is both symbolic of Their
sacred union and intended to encourage the development of
sexual attraction and therefore magickal bonding between one
Witch and the other. In circles where this heterosexual bonding is stressed less or not at all, such as in many Dianic circles,
the energy is no less available. Less exclusive relationships are
involved and same gender pairing can be used to find the
Goddess or both Her and the God within more effectively
than in heterosexual pairings, or the emphasis can be placed on
individual insight and intuitive growth.

## The Altar

Magickal tools, many common to different traditions of
Witchcraft, have both individual and generally recognized
meaning. This is extremely important. It is the nature of
Witchcraft to be non-centralized, not dogmatic. One need not
choose to study with or align herself with a particular group
and follow its teachings to the letter. The Goddess is, after all,
within, and it is from Her, within oneself, that knowledge

ultimately comes. Therefore individual interpretation of the meaning of symbols is paramount.

Understanding this importance is necessary to prevent two problems. The first is giving up of one's own power to another or to a group. Witchcraft is about autonomy and about individual strength used in unity with others, not the surrender of the one to the many. Accepting a tool or another's interpretation of its symbolism against one's best judgment is unnecessary and even regressive. The second problem is linked to the first, being the loss of personal growth or opportunity for expression because of the rejection of a symbol. For example, the ritual knife, athame, on a Witch's altar may have a number of meanings. A particular group might assign to it the symbolism of male energy and aggressive action. If the seeker accepts this meaning without self-questioning or ignores intuitive flashes about it, she has lost an opportunity for vital self-empowerment. If, on the other hand, she rejects the athame altogether, perhaps because she follows a path which does not include aspects of male energy or is totally pacifist, she may give up the chance to see other symbolism in her own tradition.

Bearing in mind the need for the seeker to investigate her own feelings and impressions of the sexual symbolism of the Witch's tools, let us explore first their general meaning. Whether one is involved in celebration of the union between the Goddess and Her masculine consort, or in finding the Goddess within mirrored in one's relationship with oneself alone or with another woman (or of the God to be found in the love between two men), the simple spark of life-giving energy is the rudiment of a tool's meaning. The simplest non-gender differentiated organism contains it. The four elements, Earth, air, fire and water, each represent an aspect of this energy and together with the spirit of the Goddess comprise a wholeness. Likewise the five-pointed star, or pentagram, holds within it the four energies of the elements crowned by the spirit and is more specifically a sort of "stick figure" of the human body. Interestingly, the lower appendages of the star may correspond to the directions of south (fire) and west (water) in the clockwise circle and are the two we use most often in talking about sexual passion, of heat and flow, for instance. The circle itself is a symbol of wholeness and of connection with others. Witness Western cultures' development of the ring as the token of matrimony. The Round Table of King Arthur meant both commitment to a common cause and individual equality between his knights. Thus our tools at their most basic level tend to represent both the individual nature of power and its potential for wholeness and unity.

Sexual meanings at this purest level of interpretation refer to the generative energy available to strengthen the solitary Witch through identification with the Goddess within, to utilization of sex magick for individual or group efforts, and to the circle for affirming the bond between respect for the one and commitment to the common purpose. No more specific sexual meaning need be applied.

The next level of interpretation does assign certain differentiated symbolism to our altar tools, generally comprising two categories, the vaginal or female and the phallic or male. A caveat here: it is easy to accept this symbolism at face value. After all, phallic symbols are derived from the recognition of the penis as a long, narrow, penetrating object, and the vagina as a round, deep, enclosing object. As a result, these symbols are often polarized into "men's symbols" or "women's symbols" and lose their more universal meaning. Women have protruding fingers, tongues, clitorises and nipples, and men have receptive mouths, navels, palms of hands and anuses. The ovum leaves the ovary and travels to meet the sperm, not in the least passive. Thus, we will use the expressions "phallic" and "vaginal" advisedly, emphasizing our mutual aspects of both female and male energy and further interpretation, such as the "active" nature of the male and "passive" or even "receptive" nature of the female may obfuscate a more universal wisdom. Be aware of this and the fact that it is rather the meeting, the harmony, that is the essence of magick and when interpreting symbolism, feel free to assign meanings without making counterproductive value judgments.

Once the seeker understands this, it can, in fact, be valuable to designate her tools as representative of the vagina or phallus. This is because the tool then becomes charged with one's recognition of its association with regenerative or creative power. The single tool can enhance a ritual or spell through its association with a single meaning. Used in combination, it increases its effectiveness exponentially. A very ancient example is the sword and chalice, most familiar in the story of the Grail, a Christian myth adapted from an earlier Pagan myth in which the tools were the spear and the Cauldron of Cerridwen. In the Grail story, in an effort to make a more primal but popular story "respectable," the victorious knight placed the sword which had wounded Jesus Christ into the cup from the Last Supper, thus reuniting two lost artifacts and returning favor and prosperity to the land. The original meaning was more obviously sexual. The spear, or phallus, of the God was placed in the cauldron, or vagina, of the Goddess to spark their combined power, to impregnate the Earth and make it fruitful. Modern Witches still use this symbolism, using the athame and chalice or cauldron to recreate this regenerative energy to empower themselves and their projects and to stimulate and direct their own use of sex magick.

Phallic and vaginal symbols may be used in various combinations to key into different suggestions. While the athame and chalice together represent heterosexual intercourse, two vaginal symbols together can represent lesbian unity or a love relationship, or, more generally, the values of sisterhood and matriarchy. "Heterosexual" symbols are not limited to women relating to men, as lesbians can use them to represent a creative energy less bound to images of childbearing.

It is commonly accepted, but not necessary, to regard round or almond-shaped, cup or bowl-like, receptive or enclosing, unifying or internal or cyclic tools and objects and the associated energies as vaginal, and those that are long and narrow, pointed and especially thrusting or projecting, penetrating or directing, or linear, and the associated energies as phallic. Most things are not so simple to assign as most combine both elements, but one may explore the possibilities. Some examples follow.

**Vaginal:**
Chalices, cauldrons or cups
Bowls
The energy of water and Earth
Wine, water, juice, menstrual blood
Salt, soil, the garden
The directions of west and north
The tarot suits of Cups and Discs, Coins or Pentacles
Broken lines in the I Ching, particularly the hexagram K'un
The Third Eye chakra, said to be the seat of female power
Indigo stones, such as lapis lazuli and sodalite
Beads
Valleys, lakes, oceans
Earth, the Moon and other spheroids
Round flowers, such as roses, and their scents
Pumpkins, melons, tomatoes, apples
The Circle
Crystal balls
Circular or undulating movement
Repetition

**Phallic:**

Athames, knives, swords

Arrows or spears[2]

Shovels or spades

Wands

Staves or sticks

The energy of air and fire

The directions of east and south

Incense and candles

The tarot suits of Wands or Batons, and Swords or Epees

Unbroken lines in the I Ching, especially the hexagram Chien

The solar plexus chakra, said to be the seat of male power

Yellow stones, such as topaz and tiger eye

Needles

Towers, columns (natural or human-made), streams and rivers

Sources of light origination, the Sun, stars,

Trees and elongated flowers, such as columbine

Bananas, cucumbers, zucchini

Lines

Linear movement

Temporary action

By turning one's own intuition to creating a harmony of these combinations, a spectrum of meaning becames available for ritual. One may also find these combinations already existing on tarot cards, in nature, in human aesthetics. Use them to embroider magickal practice with deeper and more significant symbolism, for greater effectiveness and self-empowerment. For example, burn incense on sand in a bowl, dig with a spade in the Earth, place a long crystal termination in a clam shell, or intersperse single verse songs within repetitive chants.

The following sections explore some of the many forums for finding and using sexual symbolism in ritual.

# Ritual Crafting

Rituals can be highly formalized and structured as in church services and weddings, or they can be as informal and individual as a personal habit. There is no need to follow either of these extremes. Unless one is working alone or the group with which she is working is very comfortable with one another and disinterested in structure, some sort of framework is helpful for a variety of reasons. Even the solitary Witch will find structure useful, especially for the new practitioner, as a canvas on which to paint her own conception of just what Goddess worship is. A framework is vital to ensuring that all participants understand what they are doing, why, and what might be expected of them. Language is a prime example of the need for such structure, since words take on meaning in the context of a structured sentence but rarely without it. Most Witchcraft traditions believe that certain parts of a traditional ritual, such as casting the circle, are necessary parts of all rituals, for protection, for the honor of the spirit energies present, or simply because such an element is characteristic and distinctive in Witchcraft practice and distinguishes it from other religions. Certain orders of these basic elements are accepted as being natural to the flow of understanding, of psychological response, whether natural to the human spirit or learned through artificial structures, from language itself to the established rites of patriarchal tradition. One should be careful to use these structures as helpers and not to ignore intuitive and creative additions, changes, or completely innovative possibilities, such as wordless ritual comprised completely of sound, dance, the creation of a wall mural, group or solitary meditation.

Practiced ritualists have identified some of the following elements as common and helpful to the experience of ritual. The ritual writer may want to use them, along with ideas for symbolism, seasonality, group size, and activities to put together a ritual which will best accomplish her own or her group's purpose. It is important to have a purpose, one that is clearly defined and acceptable to all who will participate, before even beginning to plan a ritual's content. The purpose may be as simple as providing psychic space for meditation or creative visualization or as complex as honoring a daughter's first menstrual period or working a healing spell for a member of the group. The ritualist will find that the agreed upon purpose makes her job much easier. Suggestions for incorporating sexual elements into ritual will follow.

## Elements of Ritual

*Convocation* — A "calling together" and an opportunity for a gathering, of people or of one's wits, before the ritual actually commences. If alone, one should take this time to relax and clear one's mind of distractions from the day, to assess the special needs or purpose of this day's magickal work. A couple or group should learn how each is feeling, what issues might be important to consider, and share news. Convocation gives the individual a chance to make the distinction between "real life" and its concerns, and the special space of magickal practice. It enhances a couple or group's ties to each other, clears the air of stress or distraction and provides a last minute chance for the ritualst to make mental changes in the ritual based on what she hears from the other(s). It is helpful to have the convocation and ritual spaces separate, to come into the ritual space only after everyone has arrived and is focused. For the solitary Witch the separate space for preparation may be a bubble bath. For a group, a large foyer or other entranceway is suitable. In either case, getting dressed or undressed for the ritual, setting up the furniture or cushions, decorating the room may be a part of the process.

*Entering Magickal Space* — This refers to both the physical room and the mental state required in ritual. In church or temple, the convocation is accomplished while the congregation enters and seats itself to the accompaniment of organ music. The priest, minister or rabbi enters, focusing the congregation's attention on her/him, and perhaps leads all in a prayer or hymn to create the sacred space. For Witches, filing into the ritual space, taking seats in a circle, holding hands and having a participant lead the rest in a grounding exercise accomplishes the same thing. Grounding is a necessary part of all meditation, ritual or other psychic space. It generally consists of deep breathing (perhaps group breathing) and a guided meditation to help participants to feel firmly rooted to the Earth. Any psychic work tends to take one's attention away from the concrete and mundane, increases alpha wave activity in the brain and generally makes it difficult to refocus after the ritual. Grounding is an important symbol in Witchcraft as well, because we value rather than deny our connection with our physical planet, and grounding is like greeting a loved one with a hug. Alone or guided in a group, grounding exercises usually encourage the ritual participant to imagine tree roots or magickal cords growing down from the base of her spine (the root chakra) and anchoring in the Earth's core. As an important part of grounding it is a good idea, especially if there are any women new to circling or if the ritual requires individual participation, to offer a brief "agenda" of the ritual once all the women are feeling grounded. Suggestions for grounding: deep breathing, joining hands in a circle, guided meditation, singing, circle dancing, group hug, the humming or intoning of mantras or random vocalizations, and spinning in place.

*Purification* — Really a second phase to creating magickal space, purification of the space and each celebrant helps to further define physical and mental space for magickal work.

Many circles combine the purification and blessing of each woman in turn with the procession from the convocation room to the ritual room. The women line up, oldest first descending to youngest (honoring the elder, combatting the negative influence of our "youth culture"), and as each passes through the curtain separating the two areas, one of the ritualists performs a blessing rite. She might circle the celebrant three times with a smudging stick of sage, then touch salt water to her body as follows, repeating:

"May your eyes be blessed (touch each eyelid) to see the Goddess in all things.

May your mouth be blessed (touch the mouth) to always speak Her truth.

May your heart be blessed (touch the chest) and warm with love.

May your hands be blessed (touch the hands) to do Her work.

May your womb be blessed (touch the celebrant's abdomen) to send forth Her limitless creativity.

May your feet be blessed (touch the feet) to walk in the paths of the Wise."

You might focus on other parts of the body, use different language and use incense for smudging and scented oils for the blessing rite. A solitary ritualist may perform the rite on herself and couples on each other. This purification may be performed after all women are in the circle, as a group or individually. In either case, the ritual space itself should be purified and blessed, perhaps by scattering salt or passing incense around behind each woman in the circle. Do the purification before the circle itself is cast, as once the ritualists begin to invoke the directions, the magick work has begun.

*Casting the Circle* — Always cast a circle, whether the magick is to be performed alone or in a group, for a simple rite or a long, elaborate one. The circle is the most central and powerful of all magickal symbols. Since ancient times it has been considered the perfect geometric construction. In ritual it serves to bring every member of a group in sight of all others. As part of our religion it reminds us that on a circular path no one can be higher or lower, farther along or behind, better or worse than another. By casting a circle, the space, in a shape profoundly sacred to the Goddess and rooted in the psyches of each one of us, becomes a temple. The cast circle provides focus, a sense of protection, and defines the ritual space to its ultimate point. Many traditions go further and avow that the cast circle provides real protection from malicious energies, whether negative feelings brought in from the mundane world or actual spirits. Whether the circle provides this more specified safety or simply makes celebrants more comfortable and at ease, the effect is the same.

The solitary may use a length of string or cord to mark off the circle, anchoring it in the middle and using the string as a compass (the type from geometry class.) Or she may make a circular quilt or cut a piece of rug. Nine feet in diameter is traditional, but any size that will fit yourself, any partners, and your altar(s) or magickal tools is sufficient. Use a directional compass to determine the exact positions of east, south, west and north. When casting the circle, celebrants in groups may pass a ritual knife, or athame, behind each one, symbolically cutting the circle off from distraction and interference. Or candles may be lit one by one in a circle, the woman at each of the directions stopping to state a welcome to the direction. A solitary may simply walk around the perimeter of the marked circle, stopping to face outward at each direction to greet it. Placing stones, candles or decorated wands representing each element at each point will help.

To invoke means "to call to," to request the presence of a spirit. To invoke the directions begin just to the east of the north point. Pass the athame or other object slowly to the east point. Stop there and state a welcome to the spirits of the east, such as:

> Spirits of the East, I/we welcome you! Powers of air, of the mind, of bird, of the imagination! Be here with me/us now!

Pass the ritual object around to the south, then west, then north, stopping at each to state a welcome. Celebrants may use a welcome similar to the formula given above or use invocations found in other books, or written or improvised by the celebrants themselves. When the ritual tool has reached the north, it may be placed on the altar or in the center of the circle. It is traditional to cast circles in a clockwise (deosil, meaning "sun-wise") direction, as the sun appeared in ancient times to circle the Earth in this direction. Therefore all positive or growth-oriented magickal work uses a clockwise circle. Opening a circle, or doing work intended to banish an unwanted influence uses a counterclockwise (widdershins) direction of motion. Marion Weinstein, in her book *Positive Magic*, says that the Earth's own energy field moves in a clockwise direction, and to go against it creates disruption. [2]

*Invocation of the Goddess* — The invocation may also invoke the God. To invoke, as in the case of the directions, means to request the attention of a spirit. The Goddess is always there, but a ritual invocation draws our attention to her. It is done with the celebrants' focus drawn both within, to the Goddess in each of us, and towards the other women in the circle. In groups with both women and men, women are often specifi-cally honored in the invocation to the Goddess, and men for the God, but I would encourage groups to honor both energies in each individual. Specific Goddesses (and Gods) might be invoked, such as Hygeia for a healing ritual or Mei Hwa when seeking strength to face a challenge. The rite might be in the form of welcomes essentially like those for the directions, or poems, chants or songs. An individual ritualist might take the persona of the Goddess and speak to the celebrants. Circle dances can be used for physical identification with the Goddess. Even silence, an opportunity to get in touch with personal feelings, can be effective.

*Magickal Work* — This is the place for the magickal work, for the accomplishment of the purpose of the ritual. There are so many possibilities that I will only list a small number:

- Healing (with laying on of hands, massage, gemstones, balancing the aura, etc.)
- Divination (tarot, I Ching, crystal gazing, astrology, shell or stone casting, Runes, etc.)
- Making charms
- Singing
- Dancing
- Trancework (meditations using guided imagery)
- Casting spells (using specialized color, candle and/or herb magick to effect a particular occurence)
- Shamanic journeying (using an ancient technique that introduces one to power animals and helpers, aided by drumming)
- Making love (to yourself or with a partner)
- Telling stories (personal, herstorical, allegorical)
- Raising a Cone of Power (consciously building energy in a cone shape intending to use it for other magickal work)
- Discussion of a given topic

Whatever is chosen, the ritualists should be certain that each woman involved knows what is expected of her, and that any desire to refrain from participation be respected. If any energy is raised, through a Cone of Power or other intense magickal work, celebrants should be instructed to draw energy from outside, from the Goddess or a celestial body such as the Sun, so as not to drain their own. To dispel that energy thoroughly afterwards, direct it outward, to the Goddess for Her use, to a loved one, to the moon or to all the Earth in general, and ground it thoroughly by placing hands, palms down, on the floor or ground, and let the energy drain away into the Earth. Such intense energy held within can make it difficult for one to "come down" after a ritual, and can "leak out" uncontrolled. It helps to provide some opportunity for celebrants to discuss their reactions to the magickal work, whether during the ritual's heart or later, to ground energy and further understanding and self-trust.

*Feasting* — Magickal work is thirsty work and can drain one of energy! Provide the traditional "cakes and wine" or any other nourishing and refreshing foods. These can be "potluck," the ritualists advising celebrants what sorts of foods and drinks to bring, such as bread on Lammas. This comfortable time serves well as a chance for friendly conversation and further grounding. Appoint someone as the timekeeper, and keep the feasting within the circle, so that celebrants will not wander off or even leave before the circle has been opened. If the circle is outside, pour a little wine or juice on the ground, and drop a chunk of bread, as a libation to the Goddess.

*Devocation of the Goddess (and God)* — To "devoke" means to send away. As noted above, the Goddess is ever-present, so you are now simply thanking her and letting her know that your attention is switching to another focus. You can use any medium such as dance, words or song to thank the Goddess for Her presence and bid Her farewell.

*Opening the Circle* — Devoke the directions as well, starting just to the north of east this time and going counterclockwise, thanking and saying farewell to each in turn, north, then west, then south, then east. Again, any medium is possible. Thank and bid each other farewell, perhaps with the traditional "Merry meet, merry part, and merry meet again! Blessed be!" and the passing of a kiss around to each celebrant. This and the previous elements of ritual serve to reclaim the ritual space as mundane space and to ground any remaining energy.

## Sexuality in Ritualcrafting

Sex itself can be a focus for the ritual, the purpose of the ritual. Ritualists should consider these three questions when creating a ritual that involves sexuality: What result am I seeking? On what levels and in what elements of a ritual can this result be effected? How comfortable will the celebrants be with both the result and the techniques I employ? Basically, there are three ways to incorporate sexuality in ritual: symbolism, discussion and making love.

Let us consider the last first, as it is both the most straightforward and the least comfortable possibility for a great number of people.

### Ritual Lovemaking

For the solitary Witch, assuming that she has accepted the premise that sexuality is a form of magick, of communion with the Goddess, masturbation will pose little or no conflict when crafting a solo ritual. No one else need be consulted nor intimidated by this use of sex in ritual. She may orient the entire ritual to a sensuous experience, taking a long, hot scented bath beforehand, preparing a seductive ritual space around her bed or satin cushions, having oils and a vibrator ready. Her self-blessing might include a good deal of stimulation of her erogenous zones, and the heart of the ritual center around making love to herself. A friend told me she once found herself on a beautiful, secluded beach on a brilliant, hot sunny day, and took the opportunity to invoke the Sun Goddess, and, as she put it, "made love to myself and the Sun." Many books on surviving as a single person in a couple-oriented society stress the importance of taking the same time to please yourself as you would a partner. Masturbation rituals, including a solo candlelit meal, fit the bill precisely.

The woman in a couple might find adding love-making to ritual barred by her partner's opposition to Witchcraft and its conventions, or by her discomfort with sexual experimentation in general. Be sensitive. Encourage, but do not pressure. Remember that, as another friend said, "making love IS a ritual!" and if your partner resists the idea entirely, let it be, and invoke the directions and Goddess to yourself. However, if your partner is a Witch and wants to observe the sacredness of sexuality, there are a number of possibilities. Many of them follow much the same formula as the solitary ritual in the preceding paragraph, or creating a specific ritual purpose beyond the lovemaking. For instance, a couple might choose to take on the personae of the Goddess and either the God or a spiritual or mortal lover. For such sabbats as Imbolc, Beltane and Summer Solstice this can be uniquely effective for invoking the sense and meaning of the holiday. A couple might take a story from mythology or one of their own making and dramatize it, such as using the Brigid fantasy from Chapter Four as a ritual for a heterosexual couple, or creating a scene drawn from the stories of the Moon Goddess Artemis and her nymph companions.

Sexuality in a group is a touchy issue and for varied reasons. All things being equal and all parties truly comfortable, there is nothing in group sex that contradicts "Harm none and do as you will," the one law of most Witchcraft. However, it is absolutely vital that all participants are completely at ease with being involved with sex in a group, whether in the form of pairing off or as the proverbial Roman orgy. I cannot be too emphatic. First of all, few will dispute that there are people who will use such a situation entirely for their own gratification and with no interest in honoring the Goddess. Thankfully, these people are few and far between. I used to believe that the only such persons would be men, but I have been enlightened otherwise since. If you are ever in a situation where a group or an individual insists that *any* act is a prerequisite to magick, and if it is uncomfortable or repugnant to you, decline firmly and with the full conviction that you are an autonomous being and should resist any such manipulation. If the group continues to pressure you, remind them of the law, "Harm none, and do as you will" and find a new group. It is gross dishonor to the Goddess to harm another in any way, and no genuine Goddess-worshipper will do it intentionally. Other reasons for giving a lot of thought to group sex when crafting a ritual include simple consideration of others who might "go along" for fear of appearing inhibited. Never, never include lovemaking in a ritual that involves minors. Honor the concern many Witches have for the public image brought about by patrifocal religions and the media that we sacrifice babies, drink blood, and hold orgies. Discretion has its value!

After considering these possibilities, if your group is insistent that all members are completely comfortable with actual lovemaking in the ritual, then "do as you will." Having two members of the group, the High Priestess and High Priest of a coven, for example, make love as representatives of the Goddess and God, as part of the Invocation or in the heart of the ritual, is a possibility. Likewise, as in the above suggestions for couples, scenes from mythology might be reenacted. A lovely story that might be dramatized to include all celebrants, paired off, is Plato's tale of the origin of soul mates, mentioned in a previous chapter. Celebrants might "bind" themselves back to back with strips of tissue paper, break apart and "tumble," somersaulting or dancing away from each other, then reunite face to face and then make love.

## Ritual Symbolism

A more comfortable, even subtle, technique for introducing awareness of the sacredness of sexuality in ritual is through symbolism. Many traditions use this form frequently and as a matter of course. Those celebrations that commemorate certain rites of passage in the relationship of the Goddess and God or in one's own life, such as handfastings (weddings), fertility rituals like Beltane, and personal traditions like anniversaries, lend themselves well to remembering the sexual element. The most common is use of sexually symbolic ritual tools, such as the athame (ritual knife) and the chalice. A typical ritual gesture is dipping the blade of the athame into the wine-filled chalice, evoking the moment of conception of all things living by the Goddess and God. More explicit images might be used, such as "fetishes," which were originally objects with specific properties imbued in them for magickal work, such as graphics depicting the Goddess in a sexual act, suggestive dancing, stories or poetry. All these are equally effective for the solitary, the couple or the group.

## Discussion of Sex in Ritual

Perhaps because some of the renewed interest in Wicce derived from the coming together of women in "consciousness raising" groups or through psychotherapeutically focused New Age workshops, many of the women's spirituality groups use discussion as ritual and ritual as discussion. My own experience of both couple and group circling was, from the start, an opportunity to use meditation and guided imagery to focus on less obvious levels of important personal issues, and a chance to share and compare my thoughts and experiences with others. This is a valuable tool for self-empowerment. The only caveat I would offer is to be sure that your rituals do not turn into meetings. Whether or not the same ostensible purpose would be served, ritual has a distinction in its ability to reach more deeply into the participants. Always frame discussion in ritual context and trappings. Combine symbolism with some time to meditate on a topic in order to "fertilize" insight. The solitary Witch might keep a journal for this purpose. Couples might use ritual as a means of keeping in touch with their relationship, as well as to support each other's self-examination. Discussion for a group brings the Goddess to the "CR" group. Examples of topics include:

○ How do I encourage or discourage my own identification with the Goddess/God? (See the Full Moon Ritual below.)
○ What attitudes toward menstruation was I taught as a young woman, and how do I carry them into the present?
○ What does it mean to be female/male to me? To my family? To my society?
○ What scares me about sexuality?
○ What pleases/displeases me in lovemaking?
○ How can I best grow in regard to my physical self-image/sex?
○ What is the best way to raise a sexually enlightened child?
○ What can I do to gain a healthier attitude toward the role of food in my life?
○ How does/do my health/health problems reflect a poor self-image/attitude toward sexuality?
○ What sexual symbolism do I/we accept in ritual/ritual tools?

Remember that in all types of ritual that both ritual and sexuality are serious AND fun. If you can neither weep nor laugh, then neither can the Goddess, inside of or out of a ritual setting. Be creative and liberal in your use of tools, activities and formulae for ritual. You know that some habits are helpful, while others are dull or even limiting. Keeping a basic format but varying elements will provide both the familiarity and repetition needed to make ritual effective and at the same time new and interesting. You will find as you continue to participate in, read about, and think about ritual that you will be constantly getting new ideas, learning new dances and chants, meeting others with their own wealth of wisdom and experiences to share. Read and talk about all sorts of traditions, Witchcraft and even patrifocal, for insights on ritual and its characteristics and the role of sexuality in it. And BE INTUITIVE! That is your strongest suit, for when you are open to your intuition, the Goddess speaks most clearly, and She is, of course, your very best guide. And She is you.

### Menarche Ritual

A daughter raised with the recognition of her own identity as the Goddess and as part of the Goddess will learn early that the functions of her body are positive and even sacred. She will have an almost matter-of-fact understanding of them, a respect for her own impending womanhood. If you and she are part of a Goddess-identified community, perhaps she will have had the opportunity to watch other daughters reach menarche, the onset of puberty and the first menstrual flow, and look forward to it herself, thereby avoiding the tension, confusion and misinformation fostered by our patrifocal society and the sanitary napkin and feminine deodorant spray industry.

The following menarche ritual is inspired by the menarche celebration of Panamanian Indian women, who venerate menarche as a bond between women and the Goddess. The ritual serves as an illustration of the art of ritual crafting with sexual cycles in mind, and offers a suggestion for a tradition to reinforce daughters' understanding of the Goddess within them.

The Afterword to this book provides further discussion of the awareness of sexuality and the Goddess and childrearing.

Menarche for an aware daughter of the Goddess will be anticipated and joyfully announced by her, so you will find it easy to commemorate it while she is still experiencing her first menses. If you have a Goddess community, contact as many of the women who have already passed menarche as you can and ask them to come to your home for the menarche ritual. If possible, include like-minded or open-minded female relatives. If you have not already had one ready for her in the expectation that your 10–13 year old daughter will have her first menses soon, obtain some item of jewelry, a ring, a pendant, a bracelet or earrings containing bloodstone, ruby or carnelion, stones that resonate with the root or belly chakra, energy centers for sexuality and menstruation. (Please don't use coral—the coral reefs are sustaining great damage thanks to humans hunting it for jewelry.) Buy a four to six foot piece of red ribbon, cord or yarn, or three of these tied together at one end so that they can be braided. If you can, plan the ritual for out-of-doors, in a secluded spot covered with low-hanging tree brances or the overhang of a hill to simulate the womb of the mother. A cave would be ideal. But if you cannot, a small room will do, such as the daughter's bedroom, dimly lit and draped with cloth to make it cave-like. If there are only the two of you, even sitting under a draped table will work quite well to simulate the womb of the Mother. If indoors, have a small amount of Earth tied up in a cloth bag. Greet your daughter's first menses with some pomp and fanfare but, of course, be sensitive to her wishes on this. Let her choose the women attending and the extent of the preparations.

As soon as the daughter announces her first menstrual flow, consult her about the menarche ritual, then suggest that she spend a good deal of the time until the ritual in meditation. Tell her to pay close attention to her dreams during this time and to write about them in a dream diary, or to use whatever artistic talent she enjoys to express her feeling and describe her dreams. Tell her that she may now choose a special name for herself, which she may keep a secret or share only with the women of the Goddess community. In the meantime, prepare the ritual yourself, with the help of women relatives, if that's feasible. Have each woman coming to the ritual bring your daughter a gift that represents what womanhood means to her. Prepare your daughter's favorite foods for the feast.

When the ritual space is ready, bring all the women together in the next room or outside the grove or cave (except your daughter who should be somewhere else nearby meditating on a name that she wishes to take to mark this time). Greet them, saying that you are meeting as a society of women, maidens, mothers and crones, to welcome your daughter into womanhood at her first bloods. Explain any special observances you have planned, or the whole ritual if you have not performed it before as a group or have new members. Stand in a circle holding hands, and simply be together for some minutes, smiling into each others' eyes, grounding individually, or singing together to reinforce the group bonding. Welcome each woman into the prepared ritual space in order of age, eldest first, blessing each one with blessing oil or salt water as follows:

> Welcome, (name), to the celebration of (daughter's name)'s first bloods! I bless you in the name of the Goddess as you enter Her Womb. (Sprinkle her with oil or water, or touch oiled or wet fingers to her breast over her heart and her abdomen over her womb. Hug her and let her pass into the ritual space.)

Have an older family member or special friend stand out to welcome and bless you. When all have entered the room or cave set aside for the celebration and have taken their places standing or seated in a circle, go to your daughter and bring her into the room. Perform a blessing on her, such as:

Welcome, my daughter, to the Womb of the Mother! I came from that Womb, as you came from mine, and I re-entered it to come forth again as a woman, as you do now, and as you may some day guide a daughter of your own into womanhood.

Bless your mind, clear and free as the soft breezes of summer. (Touch oil or water to her forehead.)

Bless your eyes, soft as a mountain lake or flashing with fire like the sun's. (Touch her eyelids.)

Bless your mouth, sweet with laughter and with anticipation of kisses to come. (Touch her lips.)

Bless your heart, brimming over with the blood of joy which now flows from your womb in womanhood. (Touch her breast over her heart.)

Bless your belly, rounding now as you leave childhood and able to grow large and full if you choose to be a mother. (Touch her navel.)

Hug her and bring her into the center of the circle or, if you are alone with her, sit across from her. Introduce her to each of the women, who should greet her and hug her.

Ask each woman to sit and to relax. Lead them in a grounding and centering meditation:

Breathe deeply and slowly. Feel the inrush of breath like a deep, cool drink of water, pouring into you and smoothing out and cleansing your insides. Feel the air you expel wash away any distracting thoughts, any tensions, any worries you bring into this space from your day. Keep breathing, deeply and slowly, feeling your body and mind relax, feeling yourself begin to drift and surge, as if each breath were actually the pull and push of gentle waves. You realize that you are lying in a large lake. Look around and see the shore, the sky, the water lapping at your skin. You are securely buoyed up and cannot sink. You remember that once, when you were above this lake, on a mountain, in a tree, flying overhead, you saw that this was not a lake at all, but the crystalline yet liquid body of a huge woman. Her skin, not resistant like a human woman's, is instead a thick, viscous, clear liquid, that a swimmer could enter and explore her body with ease. Feel her hands as they caress your limbs, buttocks, back and hair, like gentle waves. You feel utterly relaxed, utterly safe and secure.

You feel yourself drawn to this huge woman's womb, so you let yourself begin to sink. Your head fully underwater, you find you breathe easily in the fluid of her body. You swim down into the deepest part of the woman-lake, and can see as you pass through into her womb, can see that the spirit of the womb of every woman ever born, back to the one ancestral mother of us all, is so vast as to hold them all. Find the spirits of some particular woman or women, communicate wordlessly with each and share your woman wisdom. (Pause a few minutes.) You find that you are drifting out of the woman-lake's womb, through her birth canal, coming slowly into the light. When you drift up and out of the lake, you find you awaken from your meditation on the shore of the lake. You are clear, refreshed and focused on our celebration.

Cast the circle by greeting the directions, starting with the east and ending the clockwise circle at the north. Keep the circle casting simple, as the devocation of the directions will be more elaborate, perhaps saying nothing more than "Welcome, spirits of the (direction) to our joyful and loving celebration!"

To invoke the Goddess, ask each woman in the circle to speak a name of the Goddess. Chant each name several times as you dance and weave in a clockwise circle around the young girl. Tell your daughter to watch each woman as you all move and dance in a clockwise circle around her, to look for the Goddess in each, to understand from their movements the meaning behind the Goddess she chose, and to feel free to imitate them, laugh with them, speak with them. Continue to move the circle, each woman singing or humming and dancing to show how she feels about becoming the Goddess.

For the Magickal Work, all should sit around your daughter as she lies down in the middle. Hold hands in the circle and concentrate on her. Place the handful of earth in a small cloth bag on her belly. Say,

> My daughter, you are deep within the Earth, within the
> womb of your Great Mother. We, your sisters, are there
> with you, preparing you to be reborn as a woman. We have
> each made the journey, and we will lead you to your own
> womanhood.

Each woman, beginning with the eldest, should lay her hand on the bag of Earth and say a blessing, tell a reminiscence of menarche, offer an affirmation on the beauty of the bodies of women, sing a song, or otherwise send her own energy and blessing into the bag. After each has done so, all should join hands again, leaning over the daughter, and hum a chant or random notes. Separate yourself from the circle, lean over and lift the upper part of your daughter's torso to a sitting position. Hug her tightly, then release her suddenly, as the humming of the women rises to a yelp of joy, in which your daughter should join. She is here reborn as a woman! The women should touch and stroke her, smile, laugh, and greet her. Returning to places, again eldest first, each should present her with her gift, explaining its meaning. You should place the

jewelry on her, stating that it is a token of her womanhood.
Give her the red cord, instructing her to tie a knot in it each
day, braiding between the knots if three strands were used,
until her second menses arrives, to commemorate each day of
her lunar cycle. Say,

> Now you are a woman, and as a woman, you will share in
> that invention of womankind, the awareness of the passage
> of months, the calendar. Each day as you tie a knot in your
> menarche cord, feel the Goddess within you, say the name
> you have chosen into the cord, and when the first day of
> your next bloods comes, tie the last knot, count them, and
> remember that number: it is your own. You will find that
> your bloods most often will come to you in that many days.
> On that day, tie this cord around your waist to relink your
> body with the Goddess's. You are the Goddess.

Your daughter may take this time to speak, to ask questions of
the others, to announce and explain her new name. Feast
together while she does this, paying attention to her, answer-
ing her questions.

To open the circle, your daughter should go to each direction, counterclockwise starting with the north, and thank and
say farewell to them, telling what each represents to her, members of the circle adding correspondences and meanings as
they wish. Let your daughter thank and hug each woman, then
join the circle to say "Merry meet, merry part, merry meet
again! May the peace of the Goddess go with you! Blessed be!"

*By providing a* positive environment, through love and ritual, for
the daughters of your community, you will be fostering a
strength in the new generation of women who will follow these
first decades of the return to the Goddess. Instruct her both in

the traditions of your path, and in the autonomy she deserves to make her own choices, to trust her own intuition, and to find the Goddess within.

In the next section, recognizing the meaning of sexuality and identification with the Goddess in the esbats and sabbats, you will find additional opportunities for special sharing of your daughter's participation in Goddess religion and understanding of her own body.

## The Wheel of the Year

Being an Earth religion, Witchcraft centers its traditional celebrations on the rotation of our planet around the sun and on the rotation of the Earth's moon around the Earth. We have eight sabbats, or sun-related rites. The four lesser or cross-quarters are the solstices, when the sun is farthest from the equator, and the equinoxes, when the sun is directly above the equator. The cross-quarters mark the beginning of the seasons. The major sabbats are located exactly between each solstice and equinox, and celebrate each season in its fullness: Samhain, Imbolc, Beltane and Lammas. The lunar rites, or esbats, occur on the day each month when the moon is full, and there are thirteen full moons per solar year. (Thus the derivation of thirteen as the Witch's number, as the number of women in a coven.) Each lunar cycle has been given names by such cultures as the Native American, Jews, and more recently women's communities. Quite a few groups observe the New (or Hare) Moon as well, or Diana's Bow (the barest hint of the first crescent). In all, Witches have twenty-one rites per solar year, the thirteen evenly spaced esbats and the eight sabbats, each approximately a month and a half apart. Most groups observe esbats within their smaller groups, covens or circles, while sabbats are frequently community gatherings. Many conventional calendars give the dates of the moon phases and the crossquarters, and there are several Witchcraft and lunar calendars available through the pagan and feminist spiritual press. These latter and pagan periodicals are a rich source of information on appropriate symbolism for each and ideas for rituals and magickal workings, as are many books available on Witchcraft and magick. (See bibliography.)

While Witches are by no means limited to rituals on these twenty-one holidays, they are the essence of worship of the Goddess. One may wish to add other celebrations such as births, birthdays, handfastings, passings, special gatherings to work magick for peace or healing, or these may be timed to coincide with an esbat or sabbat. It is easy to design a ritual when one has a basis of traditional associations for each season to build upon. An understanding of the role of sexuality in ritual, should be used liberally with the addition of one's own intuitive and creative input. For all rites an important element is seasonality, and adding items from nature such as colorful leaves in autumn, fresh flowers in spring, a quilt spread out on the floor for deep winter, or going skyclad (nude) on a very hot day, deepens our connection to the seasons. Vegetables and fruits which are in season can be a wonderful part of holiday meals. Especially when so many of us live in cities and large towns, it is vital to bring a sense of nature within, even if only through symbolism and creative visualization.


## Esbats

We celebrate the lunar cycle at the particular request of the Goddess. This cycle represents Her own and is commemorated in women's menstrual (meaning "monthly" or "moon-ly") cycles. Esbat is the "bottom line" Witchcraft rite, supplemented by sabbats and other festivals. Esbats are sacred to women, and women are especially sacred at full and new moon. Even skeptics recognize the importance of lunar cycles on the Earth and its denizens, in the tides, on human behavior and on animals and other realms. Before the advent of electrical lighting and urbanization, the effect of the moon on menstruation was more obvious, as all the women in a community would have their flow during the same general lunar period. Women who today live alternate lifestyles, away from night lighting or traveling together, find that their cycles begin to synchronize to each other's and with the moon.

Esbat rituals focus mostly on the Goddess alone, and on women as the Earthly representatives of the Goddess. It is the time for a woman to look deep inside and to honor the Goddess she finds. (Men will want to concentrate on the Goddess within as well, although their own physical cycle seems closer to the solar flare cycle of approximately forty days than the lunar twenty-eight; each esbat is a unique opportunity for men to identify with the female energy they all possess.) Circles offer a space for this self-examination and for sharing what they discover. On an emotional and intellectual level esbats offer the opportunity to take stock on a regular basis, to judge the last month's accomplishments and to set new goals for the next.

Women readily relate to the physical lunar cycle, marked with their regular "bloods," and most can identify monthly patterns of sexual arousal and response. Even women who no longer menstruate can and have found, through the keeping of personal lunar diaries, that the cycles remain. I have noticed not only a mood cycle identical to my pre-hysterectomy menstrual cycles, but also a clear monthly pattern for both my orgasms and my body temperature. A woman's body produces hormones in its characteristic (and normal) fat layer whether or not her ovaries are functioning, and therefore is influenced by phases of the moon. Those who have not identified their own lunar cycles should keep a journal on such body patterns as menstruation, body temperature, energy and fatigue, moodiness, weight fluctuation, biorhythm, sexual arousal, orgasms, food cravings, and other features that seem to fluctuate over short periods of time. The reader probably will not find a neat, twenty-eight day pattern, but she WILL find that unique pattern which is her own, the Goddess's fingerprint in her life. Those interested in astrology or the various forms of divination will likewise observe patterns after frequent, regular exploration.

What each woman learns may be shared within a discussion group, circle or coven, and as regular self-examination of breasts and vagina are a key to preventing cancer, each woman may help the others with practical help and advice. Since the beginning of the Women's Movement, many women's health collectives have held regular self-examination clinics entirely outside of spiritual observances. Betty Dodson, author of *Liberating Masturbation*, an early Women's Movement book, held regular workshops to discuss, examine, and practice techniques for improving women's sexual self-knowledge and self-empowerment through masturbation. In ritual, female symbolism should predominate, with circles, spirals, vessels, vulva and vaginal images, blood red objects, wine and so forth. Women in the group might wish to compare orgasm patterns and take turns designing rituals based on their own unique energy flow. Solitary ritualists and women practicing with a partner might make use of the same tools for understanding the lunar cycle. Depending on the time of year some Goddesses are more or less appropriate to certain esbats, but no Goddess is ever inappropriate. Moon Goddesses, such as Selene, Artemis, Diana and Hecate are always appropriate.

Esbat is ideally suited to any self-exploration. The following ritual offers an example both of how to incorporate sexual themes into group practice and of how the reader might use the materials in this book to create a meaningful vehicle for self-understanding and identification with the Goddess.

## Full Moon Ritual for Affirming the Goddess Within
### (with thanks to Artemis Bonadea)

Participants should be asked to bring food that they associate with sensuality and pleasure, and to wear or bring sensuous fabric and scents.

The ritual space should be somewhat dim, with candlelight predominating. Have candles, if possible, at the four directions. Use a heady incense such as jasmine, or a wood-scented incense such as patchouli or sandalwood. You may want to have music playing quietly in the background to set a meditative mood.

As participants arrive, take them to a room separate from the one in which the ritual will be held. Here they are allowed to settle down and talk a bit, with a curtain obscuring their view of the ritual space. This curtain, which can be made with a white sheet, red fabric and some yarn, represents the Sheela ma Gig, a Goddess/spirit from Ireland who is always pictured sitting, with her knees up and wide apart, and her hands coming from underneath her legs to hold her labia spread apart. The curtain is cut from the bottom to the point of the Sheela ma Gig's vagina.

When it is time to begin the ritual, the women go through the slit in the curtain one by one, going "back into the womb." Once inside, they remain standing and form a circle.

*Invoke the Elements* — Give cards with the following invocations to the women standing closest to the points of the compass. If you prefer, arrange with four women before the ritual to memorize the invocations and to purposefully take the appropriate positions in the room. Starting with the East, the women read aloud:

*East:* I am the Child who stands up from the breast of
Mother Earth to gaze into the dawn. The very sight of the

first thin rays of sunlight send me careening into the morning air, laughing and singing, spinning my arms about like flailing swords.

*South:* I am the young Maiden, seeking a new lover out of the heat of the noonday sun. Whoever she or he may be today, we become as one, a human wand that kindles with flame, mirroring the great golden giant in the sky.

*West:* I am the Mother, sitting with my beloved and those creations that we nurture, whether children, animals, gardens, or our work, sharing a twilight meal. We pass around a cup of the clearest spring water, first pouring a bit onto the ground to honor the Great Mother of All.

*North:* I am the Crone, looking back from midnight over the long day of my life. As I stand on the mountaintop, feeling my feet firm on the stone and on the knowledge gained through my lives as Child, Maiden, and Mother, I still love, I still have passion, I still play, but now I also have quiet and peace. Blessed be us all.

While music is played, with recorders and drums or a record (Suggestion: "Tyme" by Robin Fre on Kay Gardner's album *Fishersdaughters*[3]) the circle moves in a clockwise direction, each dancing in free form. You may want instead, or also, to move around the circle singing or chanting. Choose songs and chants which have themes of identification with the Goddess and/or of self-nurturing. Afterwards, all may sit in a circle.

*Invoke the Goddess* — One participant, preferably one of the planners, recites the following:

We women who have gathered in a circle on this full moon to honor You, and You in us, call upon You, O Goddess, to show Yourself in your threefold image, in the world and in our own lives. Let us find each of Your thousand names written in the living diary which our own footsteps inscribe.

Maiden Goddess, not ignorant of love and passion as they would have us believe, but free and independent, pairing where You please, and full of the energy of fire! Ancient Kore, whose name can be found on temples, cities, rivers all over the Old World, honored in Egypt, Israel, Greece, Germany and Britain, the maiden also named Persephone, She who lived long before the story of Her abduction by Hades was told, You who were praised in Your own right, Solitary and Complete, be here now!

Mother Goddess, partner but never lesser to Your beloved, nurturer, creative force, from whom we all come, and from whom we manifest our own imaginations, images of You, of us, of the rocks, seas, trees, clouds, and animals of Your body! Tiamat, "The Deep," who divided Yourself into the Earth and the Sky and became the horizon, giving Your name to us as "Diameter," whose first child was Yourself, who made the world when You bled for three years and three days, Your menstrual blood still preserved in the Red Sea, You who care for us all, be here now!

Crone Goddess, returned to solitude but ever strong, You who hold knowledge, even that of the cycle of death and life, free again to find love where You want it, and to hold all the world in Your arms! Cerridwen, Kore transformed, the Sow Goddess, revered from Malta, to Norway where you reigned as Freya, who gave the knowledge of Your old age to the poets to spread across the world, honored at harvest and Yourself the harvester of souls, keeper of the great Cauldron, womb of the Earth, from which we come and to which we go, O Goddess of the circle completed, be here now!

*Work the Magick* – The same or another woman guides the following meditation:

> Close your eyes, relax and breathe deeply and evenly.
> Imagine that you are a tree growing in fertile, rich soil. Your
> roots are free to reach deep within the Earth, to anchor
> securely and to draw up nourishment from the Earth. Feel
> this life-giving fluid flowing up from the hairs on your roots
> up into your trunk, then into your limbs, branches, twigs
> and leaves. You are full of its warmth now. The sun is
> shining down on your broad, heavy crown of leaves,
> warming them further, and Her light enters them and mixes
> with the nourishment, spreading it further within you,
> making you radiant. You have so much radiance that you can
> let some of the fluid, imbued with the Sun's energy, flow
> back down to your roots to feed Mother Earth. You feel
> grounded, centered and clear.

Remember now. When you were born, all you knew was yourself and the nourishment that you received from your mother.
Then you knew her smile and her voice, and for a while it
seemed as if you knew the Goddess, and saw Her in yourself.
Then it all began to fall apart. When you ran and played hard,
you were told to be lady-like and not mess up your dress. You
saw boys get away with it and even blame you when they got
into trouble. As you grew you tried your hand at exciting new
things, like building, or numbers, or what the Mothers called
"knowledge" but what the Fathers call "science," but when you
excelled you were at best unacknowledged, at worst you were
criticized for invading the boys' world. When they talked,
others listened, admired; when you talked, you were "gabby."
When silent, you were a "regular little woman" because you
had nothing to say, and nothing to share. You ate like a bird or
you were a pig, while your brother "would be a boy" or had a
man's appetite. When you had your first bloods they didn't tell

you about the moon and your young womanhood, but instead told you to keep it a secret, to hide your tampons, to deodorize your body, to stay indoors and be quiet. When you found a good and true friend and loved her, your parents looked worried. When you asked for a bike for Christmas, your brother needed one first, for his paper route. When you got a bike, it was designed more for your "modesty," even though you wore jeans, than for efficiency or safety. When you sat in school the teacher seemed to call on you less often than the boys, and showed less interest in your answers than in theirs. And they told you about God, who was your Father in heaven, and when you found out where babies come from, you were amazed that the universe only needed a father. He must be very strong and very big. And when you grew up and tried to be independent, to be a whole woman, to study and work at what you pleased, and to love whom you wanted, to live where and how you chose, and to be respected for your life, you found that you didn't know where to start, what to say, how to prove yourself, what to do when you were prevented from doing what you wanted. You hid your life, you kept your dreams secret and you found it hard to discover the strength and ambition that others seemed to have. You are, even now, a little girl. A little, tiny, unimportant, unintinteresting, weak girl.

Breathe deeply and evenly. You are not tiny, you are not weak, you are not unimportant. You are the Goddess. You are as vast and vital and strong as the Earth. Begin to feel your breath as the rush and withdrawal of waves on a beach. Slowly begin to sway with the rhythm. You are the Goddess; you are the Earth. You can feel your almost imperceptible rotation. You can sense the chill of your night side and the radiance of the sister sun on your day. The top of your head and the bottom of your feet are faintly cold. Great oceans move with your breath; feel them. Great rivers cross your land and feed you. Your sky draws up their water and sprinkles it widely across your surface. You can look out upon your own moon, which silently circles you. Your sister planets move on their own paths. Faraway other stars are circled by their own planets. You feel the pull of each one as you in turn pull mildly on each of them. If you wish, begin to hum a tone or a succession of tones as you feel the different cycles touch you in turn. Be aware of your Earth body: sense the valleys and mountains, the forests and the deserts and the creatures scattered throughout. Feel deep inside your molten core. Feel the change in your tilt and the change it effects on your surface. Stay with the feelings for a while. Come out slowly.

The participants should take turns discussing ways in which they deny themselves, and thus deny the Goddess within. They can relate these to the first part of the meditation if they wish. They may comment on methods that they use to affirm Her, to honor her and to treat themselves with love and indulgence.

Over a feast of foods that each associates with sensual pleasure, the circle may want to talk about things that feed the senses: perfumes, colors, foods, fabrics, music and hot baths. Pass around items the women have brought which they find pleasurable. (When my own circle performed this ritual, two of us brought stuffed animals, a tiger and a mountain lion. We had them play together and they wound up getting pretty amorous!)

*Dismiss and Close the Circle* — Sing a directions chant in reverse order or simply thank each direction, North, West, South and East and say goodbye to them. The circle says, "The circle is open but unbroken-blessed be!" Pass smiles and a kiss around with a communal hug.

## Sabbats

The Wheel of the Year, one of the great circles of the Goddess, represents the movement of the Earth around the sun and the continual turning of the seasons. For most of our time on Earth, people have been directly connected to the seasons, to the climates of our thousands of different cultures, as gatherers and hunters, as farmers and grove keepers, as fishers, and later as traders and travelers. It has only been since industrialization and the urbanization of many parts of the world that the seasons have become less vital and seem simply a matter of comfort, how cold and snowy or how hot and humid. In not very much earlier times all of life centered around recognition of the meaning of the seasons, of appropriate activities for each, and of spiritual observance of the changing Earth and sky. Long before telescopes came into use people knew of the changes in the Earth, and those changes in the sky which coincided with them. Their myths reflect it, with deities for each season and stories about the changes. Their artifacts reflect it: Stonehenge, one of the most famous, marked the exact point of the Summer Solstice for the Druids.

The Wheel of the Year is significant to Witches because the changes in the Earth mirror for us the Goddess's rites of passage. We see in the turn of the Wheel Her transformation from Maiden to Mother to Crone and back to the Maiden. Different traditions identify Her phases with different times of the year, but the process and meaning are essentially the same. The various justifications for placing a phase in a particular part of the cycle are each quite valid. It is part of the nature of paganism and Witchcraft that scores of traditions with superficially different paths still converge at the same destination: the Goddess. These life cycles also relate to the lifespan of the Goddess's consort, the Horned God, although He often has two aspects, the Son and Lover, to Her three. A few traditions add the Brother as a sort of companion to the Mother and even to the Crone.

In all cases the Wheel of the Year follows the sexual maturation of the deity. Certain points in the cycle have very specific sexual references, such as May Day, or Beltane, with its commemoration of the sexual maturation of both deities and their sexual union, symbolized by that very famous phallic symbol, the Maypole. These seasonal rites of passage were directly related to the growing seasons, and in different climates progress at different rates. In warmer parts of the world celebrating planting and fertilizing symbols in May or even March might seem rather after-the-fact. These spring planting images find their way to us from northern cultures, which have shorter growing seasons. People of the southern hemisphere would have opposite calendars as far as seasonal associations would be concerned. Witches come from all these seasonal-varying religions and traditions. Which you choose will be affected by what tradition speaks most to you, where it originated, and where you live now. The following examples of the Wheel of the Year are from my own perspective, being attuned to traditions from a wide variety of origins, largely northern, and now living in the Pacific Northwest.


### Samhain

This holiday occurs on the night of October 31st and is also called Hallowmass (Feast of the Holy) and continues to be celebrated today as "Halloween." Many of its associations will be extremely familiar, however fractured and commercialized, they remain in our culture. The scary stories we tell on that night, as well as the personalities of many of the costumes worn when "trick-or-treating" are replete with Witches, otherworldly spirits, representatives of the dead. Samhain, pronounced "SAV-IN" (Irish Gaelic) or "SOW-IN" (Scots Gaelic), is the Witches New Year's Eve, marking the time when nature goes underground, and growth is temporarily put on hold awaiting the renewal of spring. The veil between the seen and unseen worlds is at its thinnest, so spirit sightings are easiest on this evening. Much magickal work, such as raising the Cone of Power, will be more intense and effective. The Goddess is fully in Her Crone aspect at this time, therefore it is sacred to Crone Goddesses, such as Hecate. Even in those traditions which recognize a threefold God, the Brother has disappeared into the womb of the Earth by Samhain. (Some traditions mark this time as the beginning of the God's guardianship of the Earth as the Goddess enters into the dark to prepare to be rejuvenated. Others do the opposite.) In Witchcraft there are no endings without beginnings, no finality to death, no originality to birth. Just as Changing Woman of the Apache walks around the Earth, growing ever older, to meet herself coming the other way as a young woman and merging into her younger form, so each ending in human life is constantly merging with another beginning, and vice versa.

Sexuality is not absent from this time of the Wheel of the Year, any more than it is absent from the lives of older people. It is simply transformed into the comfortable, companionable warmth of long love, free of the procreative urge. This time of year celebrates women who have attained menopause, whether older women or, if they so identify, women who have had their uteruses and/or ovaries removed.

Because the last crops to be harvested are usually squash and pumpkins, it is not surprising that jack-o-lanterns are carved from these. They are symbols of the light going inside, as the sunlight is declining noticeably at this time of year. My partner and I use four small pumpkins carved with facial features influenced by the characters of the four elements, air, fire, water and Earth, as the candleholders for the Guardians on our altar. Fall colors are traditional, orange, brown and black for the growing darkness. Even the tradition of giving goodies to children derives from a pagan celebration, from Italy, which leant its gift giving custom to Halloween and later to the Feast of St. Nicholas in early December, and to Christmas.

## Yule

It is no accident that the Christian religion has chosen December 25th for the date of the nativity of its child-God, Jesus Christ. The Winter Solstice which occurs a few days earlier (and probably coincided until recent calendar changes) marks the point when the days cease to shorten, and the sun seems to be "reborn." Birth, in fact, is the major image for Yule. It is the point when the Goddess transforms from Her Crone aspect to Her Maiden aspect. It is also the birthday of the God in many traditions. The apparent contradiction in the Maiden giving birth and remaining a virgin should offer no conflict for Christians, especially Catholics, as this image was translated by them into the Holy Virgin Mary and her son. The word "maiden" in Goddess tradition, however, refers more often to the Goddess's youth and to Her personality than to the preservation of Her "maidenhead." In fact, it is traditional to honor women with babies or small children on this day, and the symbolism should be extended to include women who are new in a role or career, students, apprentices and learners of all sorts. This day is sacred to Goddesses like Lucina, a Roman Goddess whose name means "light" and who is still recognized in Northern Europe as St. Lucia. In their celebrations, one of the daughters of the family wears a crown of candles and reigns over Advent festivities as Lucia.

Yule is also the celebration of the rebirth of hope, as the growing light promises spring and the renewal of the growing season. It is further a time to reconsider the negative connotations of darkness, reminding us that the diminution of the light is part of the natural process, it is necessary for the continuation of our biosphere. All through the dark the seeds are underground, waiting to sprout into the light. Thus was the God, who is often associated with the life-giving principle, in the dark when He was in the Goddess's womb. In our ritual, we burn the candle that we blessed and set aside at Imbolc to augur the waxing of the light.

Sexually, Yule is a time for new beginnings, for new relationships or phases of relationships, or for new sexual practices. The nurturing character of a maternal type of love is called forth, with a plentitude of hugging, cuddling and fondling in lovemaking. Images for Winter Solstice represent the promise of rebirth and renewal of the light and hope. Christmas abounds with them: the Christian nativity story itself, a re-telling of the birth of the child-God to the Mother; the tree, an *evergreen*, symbolizing the constancy of life and, as trees are phallic symbols, a tribute to the boy-God; candles and Yule logs remind us of the light and, along with bonfires, are kept burning the length of the shortest day. Gift opening commemorates the blessed event as well as symbolizing the disclosure of a new light or hope and promised growth. My partner and I inaugurate a moratorium on spring and garden plans on Yule, which lasts until Candlemas (early February), as a winter depression preventative. Red and green candles are traditional, red representing the God wherever He is identified with the sun and green representating growth. White candles are often used to symbolize the Maiden.

## Imbolc

Imbolc is the Celtic name for the feast which later came to be known as Candlemas. It is usually celebrated on February 2nd, not coincidentally with American Groundhog Day, with which it shares some imagery. The Roman feast of Lupercalia, which translated into the "Christian" Valentine's Day, occurred at this time as well. Again, many customs relate to both. Imbolc is the celebration of the growing, or waxing light. This date marks the exact mid-point between the shortest day at Yule and equal day and night at the Vernal Equinox. The Goddesses roam the world the night of Imbolc, looking for warm shelter and for the young God, who now enters his Lover aspect. This day is sacred to the Celtic threefold Goddess, Brigid, who is a very ancient Queen of Heaven and a Sun Goddess. It is the celebration of Her first joining with the God, which energizes the sprouting of seeds, his own seed being planted in Her at this same time. Their child will be spring itself, and auspicious preparations on our part can help bring an early spring, similar to the tradition of the groundhog not seeing its own shadow on Groundhog's Day. On Imbolc we honor all young women in their first sexual ripening, those at menarche and those in their first throes of love.

Imbolc's sexual imagery is strong and direct. One custom is to prepare a warm and inviting bed for the Goddess, stealthily hiding an athame between the sheets, thereby symbolically putting the young God into Brigid's bed. Celebrants then go outside to call the Maiden in, with tempting references to warm sheets and hot mulled wine. That night, She will visit, find the Lover in Her bed, make love to Him and be filled with the promise of spring. Friends have told me that they invite Brigid into their own bed and snuggle in close with lots of quilts against a New England winter night. We have prepared guest room beds, even sleeping bags on the floor for Her. We always have food and wine ready, reminiscent of leaving cookies and milk for Santa! In the morning we look at the bed, knowing that spring has been conceived there, as well as in every other bed prepared for Brigid. This story, being particularly suited for role-playing, is included in the next chapter as a magickal fantasy to act out. Needless to say, Imbolc is a festival of young love, and we carry on its traditions today in Valentine's Day. It is a time to find new love or to recall and reawaken those first romantic days with one's lover. The valentine shape, which we call "heart-shaped," is actually the shape of the vulva. Brigid's bed itself is a vaginal symbol. Phallic symbols are obvious as in the athame placed in that bed, as well as the candles (all the sacred and practical candles you will use for this year plus a special one set aside for use on Yule) which are ritually blessed on Imbolc/Candlemas. The candles also represent Brigid, a Sun Goddess whose name means "bright."

## Vernal Equinox

Some pagans consider the Vernal Equinox, the day the sun moves into the first sign of the Zodiac, Aries, as the first day of the New Year. It is the time of year when the return of life to the Earth becomes more apparent and when buds appear on the trees. In colder climates this is generally the time when one starts seedlings indoors for outdoor planting nearer to Beltane. In Greek myth, the Vernal Equinox is the day Persephone (Kore) returns from the Underworld to rejoin her mother, Ceres or Demeter, who joyously brings growth back to the Earth. Witches' celebrations center around enjoying the warmer weather and the making of new plans for the summer. We consider the concept of balance, as day and night are equal on this "first day of spring." So we endeavor to bring more harmony and equality into our own lives. The Vernal Equinox is sacred, of course, to Spring Goddesses, like Persephone of Greece and Marzenna of Poland, and we honor women who are either in the earliest adult years or who strive for justice and equality. It is a day to honor women who are committed to other women, whether in lesbian relationships or in non-sexual or affectional positions of service to other women, such as teaching, nursing, social work, resource sharing and networking, or the arts. The reunion of Ceres and her daughter makes this day an excellent Witches' "Mother's Day."

Likewise, the Vernal Equinox is a day to examine one's sexuality and to determine whether balance and equality, whether within one's own body image or one's partnerships, is being maintained. Meditate on your image of yourself as a sexual woman. Look for tendencies to be too hard on yourself or too ready to accept others' strictures. Take time to discuss your relationship with your partner. When you make love, concentrate on sharing, on a balance between giving and receiving pleasure. If you are alone, take time to make love to your whole body, not just seeking the quick release of orgasm. Dedicate the next six months, until the Autumnal Equinox, to realizing dreams and to making those plans for a more balanced relationship (or whatever you discuss) come true.

Vernal Equinox is for examining your health and nutrition as well, striving against extremes. And this is spring cleaning time! Clean your place, get it ready for minimum maintenance during busier summer days. Bring some greenery in. In fact, why not put your plants around your bed before you make love?

## Beltane

Like so many other Witches' holidays, vestiges of Beltane, May 1st, are still celebrated in our ostensibly non-pagan world. As a child, I used to make up little baskets of flowers on the night before May 1st and place them on friends' porches for them to find in the morning. Beltane is the celebration of First Flowering, of the appearance of wildflowers and the earliest maturing vegetables, like green onions and radishes. Around this time we see the first rewards of our hope and our work in gardens. We are thus encouraged to keep striving. The

Goddess is pregnant with life, with the summer's crops and with our own plans. We honor pregnant women on Beltane, including those "pregnant" with creativity, those skilled in all manner of arts and crafts, the graphic artist, the good cook, the successful manager and the carpenter. This feast is also dedicated to the best accomplishments of the individual. In old Europe achievement and beauty contests were held for both women and men, a sort of precursor to the County Fair, for the sake not only of encouraging effort and excellence, but to favor the Goddess with a selection of a community's most capable people to carry out her rites. Today we may take this opportunity not only to recognize the accomplishments of others, but to take stock of our own accomplishments and to celebrate our own hard work and creativity. The first day of May is sacred to Goddesses associated with lustiness, such as Astarte or Aphrodite.

Beltane may be the most obviously sexual of all the Witches' sabbats. Phallic symbolism is strong, with the traditional may-pole representing the Lover aspect of the God in His purest role as Lord Priapus, the personified erection. Because the Goddess is already pregnant, their lovemaking is entirely devoted to pleasuring themselves, and Beltane's festivities are intense and wildly passionate. Bonfires represent the intense sexuality of Beltane, the purpose of the passion is to imbue the Earth and the growing crops with all the energy of fertility possible. Maypoles, which are also tree symbols, are placed upright in the ground, festooned with flower garlands and colorful ribbons. Traditionally, the young people of a community take positions, alternating by gender, around the pole, dancing in opposite directions so that the pole is slowly encased in the weaving of the ribbons, a symbol of the enclosing of the God's penis in the Goddess's vagina. In some traditions the "winners" of the contests were given this honor, stamping their feet hard as they circled the pole to encourage fertility to stay awake. Ancient Beltane celebrations were replete with games that focused on physical and sexual contact between people at random, and for this reason it is a holiday dedicated to lovemaking restricted only by mutual interest and consent, completely outside the conventions of monogamy. Going "a-maying" meant going out on a picnic in these first warm days of spring and pairing off pretty much as one desired. (A similar custom appears at Summer Solstice.) One may observe this ancient custom by recreating it, or adapting it to one's own circumstances. For instance, celebrating the sabbat with particularly romantic and intense sex with one's partner or by acting out your first meeting or by imagining that you are both quite different people.

## Summer Solstice

This is the longest day of the year and has been the opportunity for thousands of years for long celebrations. It marks the point when days begin to shorten, and is a reminder that autumn and winter are inevitable. That weddings are often held these days in June derives from the tradition that this Solstice is the wedding day of the Goddess and God. On this day, they unite and, in some paths, He submerges into Her to be born again at Yule. He thereby lends his energy to the Earth and becomes the God of the Dying Year, sacrificing himself so that the Earth may be bountiful. A male Witch once told me that he sees this image as emblematic of the need for contemporary men to "fade into the background" and to give women back their roles lost at the onset of the patrifocal societies. Men, he said, need to go inward, into themselves and into connection with the Earth, and leave dominance behind.

Bonfires are burned from sunrise to sunrise to commemorate the last day of the sun's reign, and Sun Goddesses like Brigid and Amaterasu have the Summer Solstice as their sacred days.

On this day we honor women who are warriors, who put passion into just struggles, political women, fighters for social change on even the most local level and, since the sun is representative of the self, strong individualists, leaders, actors and others who put themselves in the public eye. Because this is the wedding day of the Goddess and the God, we also recognize women in long-standing or very close monogamous relationships, those to whom commitment to a single partner means joyful companionship rather than resignation or defeat. Thus we may also honor those men whose commitment to women is evident in their actions and words, or through sincere dedication to a particular woman. The holiday we celebrate here in the United States which most retains the customs of the old Summer Solstice is Independence Day, the Fourth of July, full of picnics and fireworks and shows of devotion to patriotism.

Summer Solstice is another lusty sabbat, passion mirroring the blaze of the bonfire. The custom, similar to going "a-maying" on Beltane, of free lovemaking on this day, which later was called St. John's Eve, resulted in the commonness of the surnames Johnson and Jones, as children born out of wedlock as a result of the festivities were designated "John's sons (or children)." This may seem to contradict the image of marriage, but for ancient Witches the point was to celebrate sexuality and fertility in the union of the divinities. One can observe the union through the making of commitments, by being handfasted (married) on this day or by spending it alone with one's partner. One may also, if alone, celebrate one's commitment to oneself or to a particularly intense interest or cause.

To commemorate the Summer Solstice, lovemaking should be as passionate as on Beltane. Male energy will be on the wane after this, so some inner exploration as to its meaning for you would be appropriate. In sex, trading roles, whatever they may be for you, is enlightening.

# Lammas

Generally celebrated on the second of August, Lammas (Celtic Lughnasadh) translates to "loaf-feast" and has always been a celebration of the first grain harvest. Christianity was not the first religion to regard grain and bread as "the staff of life." Besides its importance in a simple, natural diet, bread itself has strong associations with the human body, and the loaf coming out of an oven with birth. The Goddess gives birth to the first harvest on this day and, since the God has lent some of his energy to that harvest, a precursor to transubstantiation of the God's flesh into bread is clear. Whether a tradition sees the God as within the Earth or as the Brother of the Goddess, She reigns alone over the harvest. Lammas is the sacred day of Earth Goddesses like Ceres, who gave her name to the food we call "cereal." This is the day to make bread truly from scratch, especially if you never have before, even grinding the grain for flour if you can. Those women who seem to be able to make "something out of nothing" are honored on Lammas, farmers, conservers, weavers, and, of course, bakers. Very practical women share the honors, those who are always in the ranks of causes or groups, those who do the drudgery and without whom others could not continue their own work.

Lammas can best be commemorated with sexual symbolism rather than actual sexual activity, or with solitary lovemaking. This is because it is the first Sabbat when the Goddess is entirely alone, the male energy having submerged into the Earth. Symbols of fertility abound in the spears of grain, which are phallic, while the grain kernel itself, the bread made from it and the oven in which it is made are more obviously female. Of course, one need not and should not refrain from sex with a partner the whole time the Goddess is alone, but as part of the observance of the sabbat and in ritual itself abstinence makes its own point. Delight the senses in other ways instead, with fresh-baked bread and butter, a pre-harvest picnic on a hillside, or even an early "Thanksgiving" dinner. The crops are not fully in, so this respite will be welcome and as a rite will serve to send further energy into the Earth or into our own plans and dreams. Lammas is, like Yule, a birth rite, and highlights recognition of how one's own efforts turn into accomplishment.

Autumn Equinox

The protype of more recent celebrations, such as Thanksgiving, this harvest festival is also called Mabon. Whatever was planted at Spring Equinox, plants or desires, comes to fruition on this day. One should look at one's present circumstances, ideas, feelings and spirit at Autumn Equinox and endeavor to trace them back to see what it was in March that led to them. Thereby, one can begin to see how both positive and negative thoughts and wishes are affirmed and made into reality by the power that we raise. The Jewish Day of Atonement occurs near this time, and it is their tradition to take this opportunity to look back over the year and assess their own progress.

In agrarian cultures Autumn Equinox marked a time of rejoicing for a growing season that was well over and its bounty well harvested and stored. For non-gardeners a fitting observance would be to take some extra time, money and effort to stock up on staples, to read about storage techniques for root cellar vegetables and fruits, such as apples, squash and potatoes, and to try to recreate that aspect at least of the harvest. This will serve three purposes besides teaching valuable skills: one acquires a well-stocked pantry, and a fuller sense of the meaning of plenty, and of "giving of thanks" to the Goddess.

Autumn Equinox is a good day to begin to prepare oneself, one's clothes, and one's home for the winter. This day is sacred to Goddesses of plenty, like Habondia, whose name gave us our word "abundance." The women we honor today are ourselves, whoever we may be, with an eye toward identifying that abundance in ourselves. It is a good day to write 20 things you like about yourself.

Although in many traditions the Goddess is still alone on Autumn Equinox, sexuality can and should be part of one's observance of harvest. This is the day to do all those things that one loves best to do, in or out of lovemaking, to feel mature and secure, and to relax and enjoy. A feast of all things newly picked from the garden or appearing on the store's shelves is in order, and the larger the crowd around the table, the better! If any day of the year is suitable for sharing lovemaking with more than one person at the same time, if one is so inclined, this is it, as the abundance of love and pleasure will be a strong and empowering symbol.

*Pagan and Witchcraft* traditions vary from group to group, depending on the geographical origin of the group's chosen path and the extent to which these traditions have assimilated patrifocal values. Thus, not all will agree with the associations and symbols I have presented above. Other than "Harm none, and do as you will," there are no rules and the reader should feel quite free to rearrange, add, subtract, embellish or utterly reinterpret the observances which come from my own celebrations and the extrapolations I have made from the symbolism which speaks most strongly to me. My partner and I are farmsteaders at heart, so we try to recall the agrarian rites, and we find that this helps to keep us in touch with the essence of a "nature religion" such as Witchcraft. The reader may find that so as well. She should do as much reading as she can in a wide variety of books and magazines on paganism and Witchcraft to glean the truest meanings and symbols for herself.

Now that we understand the nature of ritual and the calendar around which our celebrations may be based, as well as the intrinsic symbolism of sexuality and creativity in them, let us explore some special techniques for expressing this energy within those frameworks. You may want to use some of the ideas in Chapter 4 about creating sacred space and props for lovemaking in your rituals as well.

## Sacred Dance

Dance was the first ritual. Movement is the natural medium of the body. Even in our less spontaneous behavior today, we often express strong emotions through unusual physical responses. We jump if startled, clench our fists in anger or shudder with pleasure. Since the ancients made no distinction between the physical and the spiritual, relating certain formalized motions to interaction with the divine was a simple step. They added the movements they saw in nature to their repetition of common bodily emotional responses, movements like the swaying of trees in the wind, the characteristic leap or scurry of an animal and the sweep of the moon across the sky. These early ritualists believed that their symbolic actions interacted with the environment upon which they depended. They created dances to bring good fortune to the hunt, mimicking the walk of an animal and acting out the hunt itself, or they encouraged grain to grow swiftly and tall by standing in the field and leaping as high as they could.

It is the nature of repetitive body movement to draw one into a meditative or even trance-like state. Early humans saw this state as being at one with the Goddess or the God. This intense spiritual state augmented the magick meant to bring protection for the group's survival. Even a spectator was likely to be drawn into the meditative mood, to become hypnotized by the steady motion, but these early initiatory dances were not intended to be performances. We are very sensitive to others' bodies and actions: we tend to follow another's yawn with our own and to have sympathetic pains. It is difficult not to tap our feet to lively music. With the added attraction of the mutual trance state, this sensitivity drew the rest of the gathering to join the dancer in ritual dance.

Ancient people did not polarize the Goddess into "good" and "bad." They did not define her actions solely by their benefit to themselves as human beings. Thus She was the bringer of both plenty and drought, of health and sickness and of birth and death. It was not until patrifocal religions began to make vivid distinctions not only between male and female but also between those characteristics they assigned to each that humans developed the notion of separate deities of good and evil, such as the Christian Jehovah and Satan. The body became the province of the powerful and terrible female energy and was therefore associated with uncontrollable demonic forces. The power of dance to intensify both the sensations of the body and identification with the deities became dangerous. While dance is common to all primitive ritual, it has all but disappeared in modern father-God religions. It survives in Christianity only as the random gyrations of pentecostal inspiration, which the adherents would never refer to as dance.

An effect of our estrangement from our bodies and our self-consciousness about displaying them is that dance has been entirely secularized and, for many of us has become an art form to watch but rarely participate in. Witches are in the ironic position of being shy about and simply not knowing how to incorporate into our ritual that practice which once entirely comprised it. That this situation seems to parallel our attitude about sexuality in ritual is no accident. Note that certain Protestant sects ban dance altogether as a lewd practice, one that encourages promiscuity. Herein lies part of the solution to both problems, of how to incorporate sex and dance into our magickal practice and how to free the Goddess's presence in our bodies. Observance of our own sexuality can lend form and energy to ritual dance, and ritual dance can grant expression to our sexuality in the Circle.

The first human ritualists used dance to propitiate hunting, gathering and agriculture, and to mark the seasons of both the world and their own lives. They aroused the Mother Earth by stamping their feet on the ground, still a common feature of folk dance and that archetypal fertility rite, the maypole dance. They observed the mating dances of animals and imitated them. They encouraged crop growth with leaping and reaching upward with their whole bodies. They recognized the role of the moon in women's monthly cycles and honored her in their dance. They acted out their own creation myths by recreating the movements of a woman in labor. They used the movements of the body, accentuating sexual organs, to identify with and represent the generative aspects of the Goddess and God. These are elements that we may use to create our own ritual dances.

A potent symbol for Witches, as we have already noted, is the Circle, whether in its own meaning or as the form our gatherings take. Dance is the Circle in motion, the Circle and its relationships expressed without words. A first effort at bringing dance into magickal practice might be simply to take hands and walk in a clockwise direction, adding running, skipping, arm swinging, or other comfortable movements, many of which we can draw from our childhood games, like "Ring Around the Rosy." Find books on primitive or folk dance and learn such formalized but universal dance steps as the weaving step. Using a predetermined pattern will underline and strengthen your connection as a group, but do not ignore the opportunity for individual expression. Allow ritual dance to grow in this way, but do not concentrate on skill or aesthetics. Let the repetitive motion lull you into meditation. Feel the universal rhythms in the movements of your body. Let it, and the Goddess within, guide you.

You will note that most of the observances of primitive ritual dance concerned fertility. Many were specifically sexual. In some cultures, even today, frenzied dance can build up overwhelming sexual excitement, culminating in an orgasmic release of psychic energy or sometimes in communal lovemaking. As recently as the Renaissance, our own western cultures had the custom of community dances on May Day and Summer Solstice/St. John's Eve, which generally ended in couples wandering off together.

Folk dance abounds in more subtle sexual reference, more clearly in the abdominal gyrations of the bellydancer, less so in stylized American courtship dances. Popular dances of this century have reclaimed some of the more overt dance steps. Modern theatrical dance has pointedly pursued representation of sexuality. Today we may make use of both the arousal inherent in dance and the sexual meaning in certain forms of dance drawn from any of the above sources. Whatever you choose to do, allow your intuition and individuality room to express itself. Liberally intertwine choreographed circle dances with whatever steps and movements come from within your own psyche and body. Let Her express Herself uniquely in you.

Here are some suggestions for incorporating dance and sexuality into your solitary or group rituals:

○ Use meditation as a start for solitary dance ritual. Firmly ground yourself and then carry your meditative state up into a standing position, beginning to sway and then move. Use quiet instrumental music to encourage your body to move, but feel free to add other types as the mood suits, or use no music at all. Let your own rhythm express itself in silence, or let natural sounds be your music, whether live or from recordings like the *Environments* series. [4]

- Use the Circle in motion as a dance. Take turns directing the dance, either with the leader inside or as part of the Circle.
- Use drums, rattles and finger cymbals to provide a steady, driving rhythm to your dance. Depending on the composition of your group, you might want to imitate the rhythm of your own sexual expression. In mixed female and male groups, a counterpoint can be created between the building and thrusting male rhythms and the repeatedly waxing, exploding and waning female rhythms. Trade rhythms to experience the Goddess within the men and the God within the women.
- Focus the center of dance motions on your genitals, breasts, abdomen, groin, buttocks and other individual erogenous zones. Concentrate on the lower three chakras, especially the ones at the base of your spine and below your navel. They are charged with sexual energy. Primitive African dances center in this region. Move erotically. Imitate lovemaking.
- Do an all-dance, wordless ritual.
- Use hand and head gestures representing sexual activity or reminiscent of them.
- Watch films of courtship dances of animals. Birds, such as cranes, peahens and penguins are especially expressive. Their dances include vocalizing to the sky, stretching their necks out, wings flapping, coiling bodies or wings around each other and displaying tails or genitals. Imitate them.
- Use dance rituals with your lover to lead to lovemaking. Use it both as magick and as foreplay.
- Use body paint, erotic costuming, masks and sexually symbolic props to enhance your sacred dance.
- Make liberal use of both improvisational and choreographed dance rituals.
- Use physical limitations as part of the dance, not an exclusion from it. If your Circle includes a wheelchair user, try having the whole Circle sit and dance with just the upper torso or the head. Use only the rhythm of a deep drumbeat or stamping

feet to share with a hearing-impaired celebrant, and do locked arm circle dances to help guide a blind or partially sighted person.

○ Use myths or archetypes to give a story line to ritual dance. This was the first drama.

The following is a partially choreographed ritual dance for a couple. Add to it anything you feel is suitable. Alter it to your own use, changing roles, gender of the participants, elements of the dance, costumes or music.

### The Lovers: A Ritual Dance for Two

Dancers represent Pan and the Maiden, or any other archetypal pair. Go skyclad, using body makeup to accentuate breasts, groin, and extremities or use costumes appropriate to characters. Lightweight eye masks or full-face papier mache masks add both their effect and an opportunity for more self-conscious Witches to hide embarrassment. Music can consist of drums, rattles and finger cymbals played by the participants, but a recording of these or music will free their hands. New Age music that is slow and has a vivid and energetic beat will be best. A recommended recording is Kay Gardner's *A Rainbow Path.*[5] Maurice Ravel's "Bolero" is a recognizably sexual classical work. International folk music abounds in suitable melodies, particularly Native American, Asian Indian and Arabic music. Nature recordings, especially ocean surf sounds, are ideal.

Set up your sacred space as usual, with red or purple candles and strong, even musky incense. Annoint yourselves with jasmine or musk oil. Turn on the music, or begin to tap out a slow, steady rhythm on your instruments. Face toward the altar or candles, standing with your feet together and arms down. The man should be on the woman's right. Close your eyes and breath deeply, in time to the music. When you feel centered open your eyes, turn to face the other, and sway slightly as you wait for the other to open her/his eyes. Sway together briefly. Bring your own hands together in front of you, as if in prayer. Try to pace your motions to the music or nature sounds. Turn your hands to point toward the ground. Undulating with the rhythm of your swaying, bend your knees outward so that you sink toward the floor. When the tips of your fingers touch the ground, pause, and then begin to rise. As you reach a standing position, turn the tips of your fingers upward, and stretch your arms and your whole bodies up. Pause. Repeat a few times with the music. Both turn to the east and move your arms outward in an all-encompassing, rounded motion, and simulate the wafting of breezes or flapping of wings. Turn to the south and repeat the gesture, with overtones of leaping flames this time. Turn to the west and repeat the rounded motion with the arms, undulating them like flowing water. Turn to face north. Follow the arm gesture by placing both hands in front of you, palms downward, in a jerking motion, as if they had encountered hard Earth. You have grounded yourself and created the Circle with dance.

Invoke the Goddess and God within you. The man should bow on one knee with arms outstretched to the woman, then the woman to the man. Both should repeat the gesture simultaneously, with arms upward to invoke the deities outside them. Stand, place your hands palm outward, almost, but not quite, touching the other's. Circle your hands together slowly, one set at a time. With hands still close but not touching, move in a clockwise circle, take two steps to each compass point, pause, then repeat for eight steps altogether to complete the circle. Lower the hands toward the altar (this should be to the woman's left and the man's right). The woman should raise her hand to the sky and draw in power from the sun or moon. She should move as her body dictates as the power flows through her to her right hand. Both should focus their eyes on their almost-touching palms as the power flows from her to him. He should move as his body dictates as the power moves through him to his right hand. He should send the power from that hand into the Earth. Place both sets of hands together as before. Move in another clockwise circle. Stop and gaze on one another, swaying and training your eyes on the other's body lovingly and longingly.

A danced blessing follows, as the couple drops hands. The woman steps forward, again almost but not quite touching, hands and lips a fraction of an inch away from the skin, she cups the man's forehead and kisses it, then each of his eyes, his ears, his mouth, his chest over his heart, the base of his penis and his feet. The man reciprocates with the woman's forehead, eyes, ears, mouth, her chest over her heart, her lower abdomen over her womb and her feet. You may prefer to do the seven chakras instead.

Now begin to improvise, moving around each other, using feet as well as body and hands, to reach around or circle one another, always clockwise. Keep the rhythm of the drum, music or surf in mind. Gradually focus on erotic movements and brush towards each other's sexual organs. As the energy builds, begin to simulate sex. The man may want to kneel before the woman and simulate cunnilingus as she spreads her legs slightly and rotates her pelvis in pleasure. The woman should freely express her own building arousal with movements or sounds that express her unique sexuality. She might want to simulate her orgasm in dance during this phase of the ritual, expressing her ecstasy through shudders and jerks, or through spinning, sending the energy out into the universe. Or she may save it for a mutual explosion of energy.

The man should rise now or the woman should kneel. Taking whatever position the couple wishes, facing one another or back to front, he should begin to thrust his groin toward the woman's to the beat of the music. You may want to note that Ravel's "Bolero" has an orgasmic ending, and you might want to time your simulated outburst of raised energy with it. The couple can express ecstasy vocally and physically with broad gestures, quick jerking motions and intensifying moans. At the point of the highest pitch of raised energy, both shake, sway wildly, stretch their arms up, shriek, demonstrate an outpouring of power into the universe and then collapse on the ground, bellies and palms pressed hard against it. Let the energy drain thoroughly into the Earth.

After you are both fully recovered, reverse the dance to each direction, starting with the north. Raise your arms in thanks to the Goddess. Hug (touching now) and kiss each other, all smiles. Blow out the candle. Make love.

### Sacred Drama

Where sacred dance concentrates magick in movement and puts the Circle and its ritual in motion, sacred drama adds stories. Ritual theatre, whether simply for women seeking the Goddess in a group or circle, or for an audience as well, can bring to life the images and tales of both the Goddess Herself and our own ancient past, which we have hitherto held only in our imaginations. Using the visual and sound effects available to drama, the actors can create for themselves and others an atmosphere which both recreates the other times or planes of reality, and fashions a bridge between contemporary women and our herstory. For performers and audience the portrayal of Goddesses, ancient figures and archetypes offers an opportunity for immediate identification with each character. It is a valuable tool for self-transformation, and can be used with a male circle or audience members as well to help them overcome resistance to finding the Goddess within.

Since our ancient ancestors did not differentiate between

spiritual and mundane life, it was through ritual that drama evolved. The first were probably portrayals of deities and elemental forces in the context of the community's survival. By the time drama came to be written down, myths were a common subject, along with fables intended to teach a lesson. Witches today may draw from a wide variety of myths, legends and stories from around the world to reclaim the ancient use of sacred drama: to represent and thereby involve the actors and audience in the symbols and stories.

The individual or circle may utilize ritual theatre as a technique for identification with and exploration of our roots. The plays may be geared to specific observances, such as the sabbats or to significant events in an individual's or the community's life, such as a birth, the formation of a coven, the dedication of a new meeting space or a festival. The drama may be drawn from existing myths or entirely from the perceptions and imagination of the artists involved, or indeed a synthesis of both. The important thing to remember is that the writers, the performers, and the other artists involved should be open to their own intuition in the dramatic creation, and that there should be some opportunity for the audience, if there is one, to interact.

Sacred drama consists of a story, which may be written out in its entirety, set down only as a guideline for improvisation or, perhaps most powerfully, framed so as to incorporate both a script and room for the performers' and even the audience's improvisations. The play is most effective if some or all of the following techniques are used:

- Some circularity of time and place; for instance, ancient and contemporary women in conversation with one another.
- Repetitive use of language and image, chanting, random vocalization.
- Music or drumming to enhance the chanting.

- Costuming, makeup, props and sets which both evoke the character, time and place, and contain elements of everyday life.
- Papier mache or other types of masks can replace or augment costumes, adding a primitive and elemental atmosphere. They are also useful if actors play more than one character in a play.
- Ritual itself, both within the play and as a technique for writers, performers, artists, even the audience to become further involved in the dramatic representation.
- Techniques to allow the audience to determine the plot or elements of the play, including any ritual performed in it.

Sex magick holds a rich store of possibilities for sacred drama. First, building psychic sexual energy in the performance as one does in ritual itself will enhance the performers' and audience's experience of the play. Themes can focus on creation myths, on sexual rites of passage or on legendary love stories. Sexual archetypes, the Lover, the Mother, the Temple Priestess, can draw audience imagination. Symbols drawn from the recognition of sexuality as a basic vital impulse, like those we use in magick, can adorn the script, costuming, masks and props. Rhythmic drumming or chanting can imitate heartbeat, birth or orgasmic contractions, or natural sounds, like the surge of the ocean or animals' mating calls. Specifically erotic sacred dance can augment this.

Writers and actors will find it useful to make use of meditations similar to those for identification with the Goddess to add to their own understanding of both setting and character. The writer might wish to spend considerable time with all the characters in the play to enliven and individualize them, perhaps even taking them out of the context of the play into other more mundane circumstances to broaden her insights. In her meditation she might add extraneous characters or women she admires in the arts or herstory to gain an objective response to her work. Set and costume designers should use visualizations of the times and locations. Actors can focus specifically on their characters, likewise taking them out of the context of the play into other possible situations in their lives to establish a wider sense of personality. Actors may wish to get together in pairs or larger groups to share and roleplay these other circumstances. By so doing the performer strengthens her ability to improvise appropriately for the character and situation, and has the bonus of identifying herself with the Goddess or a different localization of Her than she has thus far experienced.

The following are samples of ritual theatre which the reader may use both in their present form or as a starting point for creating her own. Be sure to add as much of yourself and the other participants as feels right. Be resourceful and creative with the costumes, settings and stage props: they need not be elaborate or expensive. You need not have the same number of players as characters since roles may be interchanged. In fact, it may prove valuable to have each participant in the play try on other roles to increase each woman's opportunity to gain from participation. Use what you have on hand, and you will add an extra sense of contemporary reality for yourselves and the audience.


## Creation

It would be ideal to have thirteen actors who each play a member of THE CIRCLE and also one or more of the other characters. To this end, we suggest the use of ritual masks.

**Characters**
**The Circle** (3 to 13 contemporary female and/or male Witches, including the **Witch**)
**Cosmos/Crone**
**Maidens/Suns:** Sol and Polaris

**Mother Earth**
**First Life** (two same gender actors)
**Plants and Animals** (assorted—see below)
**The Woman**
**The Lover** (female or male)

**Set:** The backdrop should be black, dark blue or purple, with tiny metallic stars. At right are three full-length mirrors set up at slight angles to each other and arranged so that performers and props on the right will be reflected, but not those on the left.

(Curtain. The stage is completely dark. In front in a small circle of light made by a candle in the center sits **The Circle**, 3 to 13 witches dressed in the everyday clothing. They are holding hands and chanting quietly, slowly concentrating on a steady rhythm and using the opportunity to ground and center themselves. After a few minutes, as the others continue one of the women, seated at the left, drops the hands of those seated on either side of her, raises her own, and calls toward the ceiling, with her eyes closed.)

**Witch:** Great Goddess, Diana, Astarte, Cerridwen, She of the Thousand Names and Aspects! We are here in your Circle. Your children have called upon the Four to guide us in your service!

**Circle:** (calling out and then repeating the words in the melody of the chant) The East!

**Witch:** Air! Dawn! The Sword! The Arrow! The infant!

**Circle:** (as above) The South!

**Witch:** Fire! Midday! The Wand! The Sacred Pipe! The Maiden!

**Circle:** (as above) The West!

**Witch:** Water! Evening! The Cup! The Medicine Bowl! The Mature Woman!

**Circle:** (as above) The North!

**Witch:** Earth! Midnight! The Pentacle! The Trade Beads! The Crone!

**Circle:** (as above) The Goddess!

(Offstage a drumbeat begins in rhythm with the chant, slow and steady, and continues.)

**Witch:** Life initiator, Mother! We call on you to show us the wonders of your Womb!

**Circle:** (slowly and repetitively) Goddess! Goddess! Goddess!

(All lean forward to extinguish the candle. They leave the stage, chanting the word "Goddess" more and more quietly, then ceasing. The **Cosmos/Crone**, wearing a voluminous black cloak whose hood covers all of her head except for her face takes her place in the center of the stage. The **Maidens/Suns** are each hidden inside her cloak, under her arms. The **Cosmos/Crone** is holding a single white candle in front of her chest and, after a few moments, lights it so that it illuminates only her face. The drummer shakes a rattle or hits a cymbal or small gong. She slowly places the candle on the floor in front of her, and steps back from it. She lifts her arms so that her cloak is spread out completely, and begins to spin in a clockwise direction in time to the drumbeat. Abruptly, and accompanied by another shake of the rattle, the **Maidens/Suns** spin out from under the cloak. They are dressed in white, yellow, light blue and red. The stage lights come up the moment they appear. The **Maidens/Suns** laugh merrily and spin around each other playfully, moving to the right so that they are reflected in the mirrors, creating many **Maidens/Suns.** The **Cosmos/Crone** backs offstage.)

**Sol**: Sister!

**Polaris**: (echoing) Sister! Sister!

**Sol**: Sisters!

**Polaris** and voices offstage: (echoing) Sisters! Sisters! Sisters!

**Sol**: This is our time, the youth of the universe. Let us spin and dance, weaving the power of our Mother Cosmos, our bodies the warp upon which the worlds will be woven!

**Polaris** and voices offstage: (echoing) Worlds will be woven . . . worlds will be woven . . .

**Sol**: Let the Maidens, the thousand sisters, take our places in the thousand spirals, the galaxies, drawing to us the primal power until we ourselves must burst with life! We shall then bathe our infant worlds with our own radiance, and though we remain void of all but virgin heat and brilliance, may we nurture them and grant them fertility!

**Polaris** (still accompanied by voices offstage and drifting offstage at the right while **Sol** moves to spin in the middle between the mirrors). Grant them fertility . . . grant them fertility . . .

(**Sol** is alone onstage. She spins in her place, showing by her movements of arms, face and body that she is experiencing her body with sexual intensity. The drumbeats pick up speed somewhat, and **Sol** spins in time. Her physical tension and concentration increases as she chants.)

**Sol**: (chanting) Mercury! Venus! Earth! Mars! Jupiter! Saturn! Uranus! Neptune! Pluto! Mercury! Venus! Earth! Mars! Jupiter! Saturn! Uranus! Neptune! Pluto! My own worlds! My own worlds! (She opens her eyes wide and begins to shake her arms in the air in time to the drum.) Earth! Earth! Earth! Earth!

(She continues to chant the word "Earth" as voices offstage take up the chant. Their combined voices increase in volume slowly. Abruptly, **Mother Earth** bursts forth from between two of the mirrors. She is dressed in green, blue and brown, with a small white "skullcap" and white shoes. Her full skirt is floor-length and full, and she has blue scarves hidden under it. She is pregnant. If the actor is not dark-skinned, her mask or makeup should be ruddy-brown. At the same point as she bursts into view, the combined voices shout "Earth!" and cease, and the drummer shakes the rattle. The drummer slows and quiets the drumbeat. **Sol** ceases to spin. **Mother Earth** slowly circles her clockwise three or four times. Then she advances downstage slowly while **Sol** stands off to the left, out of the mirrors. **Mother Earth** holds her shoulders and arms forward. Quiet, meditative music begins offstage, and the drummer matches its slow beat. **Mother Earth** sways, then undulates her body in time to the music, slowly opening her arms. She dances erotically to the music. A chair made into a birthing stool, with part of the seat cut away, is handed to **Sol**. She slowly advances behind **Mother Earth**, and then places the chair behind her. **Mother Earth** looks up into **Sol**'s face, and they gaze at one another while **Mother Earth** still dances. After a final circling of both **Sol** and the chair and two or three clockwise spins in front of the chair, **Mother Earth** sits down in it and slouches back so that her knees, which are spread, are thrust toward the audience. While **Sol** slowly moves around to kneel in front of **Mother Earth**, **Polaris** and the **Witch** come onstage and kneel on either side of her. The stage lighting shrinks to illuminate only these four. The position of the kneeling actors and the narrowed light hides **First Life**, the **Plants**, **Animals**, **The Woman**, and **The Lover** as they move into position, one by one, between the kneelers and **Mother Earth**. **Mother Earth** begins to writhe her body as if in labor. She moans. The three kneelers hum a single tone.)

**Mother Earth:** (with a cry of mixed pain and joy) My child, the Sea!

(**Sol** draws the blue scarves out from under **Mother Earth's** skirt and drapes them over and around her to represent oceans. **Mother Earth** continues to writhe and moan. With each "birth cry," the drummer shakes the rattle and continues the slow drumbeat.)

**Mother Earth:** (with a cry) My child, First Life!

(The two actors who play **First Life**, who were crouching, hands and fingers enterwined in each other's, between **Mother Earth's** legs, stand, apparently lifted up by **Sol**, and move around to between the kneelers and the audience. They spin slowly, gradually loosing their hands so that they spin away from each other offstage.)

**Mother Earth:** (with a cry) My children, the plants!

(One or more actors dressed in green, who were crouched between **Mother Earth's** legs, stand and move around between the kneelers and the audience. As the **Animals** and **The Woman** are "born" they move slowly offstage, swaying.)

**Mother Earth:** (with a cry) My children, the animals!

(One or more actors costumed as various animals, preferably a fish, a bird and a land animal, follow the actions of the **Plants**, moving appropriately for their characters.)

**Mother Earth:** (with a shout of triumph) My child, Woman!

(**The Woman**, dressed in plain modern clothing and who was crouching between **Mother Earth's** knees, facing her, half stands and leans forward to lie across **Mother Earth's** breast. They embrace each other, laughing and crying joyously. **Mother Earth** kisses and caresses **The Woman**. Slowly, **The**

**Woman** stands and moves slightly to one side, facing offstage. She holds **Mother Earth's** hand, smiles at her and then looks down to between **Mother Earth's** legs. The **Woman** smiles and reaches down, drawing up **The Lover**—who can be male or female—who had been crouching between **Mother Earth's** legs. She holds her/him at arms' length. They smile lovingly into each other's faces, then at **Mother Earth**. As **Mother Earth** stands, the kneelers stand and take **Mother Earth's** chair offstage. She then puts her arms around both **The Woman** and **The Lover**, drawing them closer to each other. She steps back, letting go, and moves back and then offstage.)

**The Woman:** My beloved.

**The Lover:** My beloved.

(**The Woman** and **The Lover** hold and caress each other. They move apart, always keeping contact by at least holding hands. They circle around each other, hold hands and circle, come back together to embrace and caress. They kneel, kiss and then lie down. They continue to move their bodies together. As they do, **Sol** and **Mother Earth** come to stand behind them. **Cosmos/Crone** comes up behind them, spreading her cloak wide. **The Woman** and **The Lover** slowly stand. The music fades and the drumbeat becomes louder. The remaining actors, again dressed as members of **The Circle**, come onstage behind **Cosmos/Crone** and slip around in front of her, one by one.)

**The Woman** and **The Lover:** (facing the audience) Our creations!

(**The Woman** and **The Lover** draw the members of **The Circle** forward between **Sol** and **Mother Earth**. Each member of **The Circle** hugs both **The Woman** and **The Lover** and steps forward to present herself to the audience as **The Woman** calls out a name. These names should include "The Child" and the names of various art forms, such as "Music," "Painting," "Poetry" and "The Quilt," trying to cover a wide variety. **The Circle** returns to its position in front of the stage. One lights a candle in the middle. **The Woman** and **The Lover** join them. **Sol**, **Mother Earth**, and **Cosmos/Crone** remove their costumes and sit in their contemporary costumes with the rest of **The Circle**. The lights on stage dim and go out. In tempo with the drumbeat—the drummer may come onstage at this point—they chant:)

**Circle:** (chanting) Goddess! Goddess! Goddess!

(They continue the chant for some moments, then raise their arms.)

**Circle:** I AM THE GODDESS!

(They point to the audience.)

**Circle:** YOU ARE THE GODDESS!

(They pass a kiss around the circle. Then each stands and, as the house lights come up, walks up to various members of the audience, placing a hand on the person's shoulder and saying to her or him, "You are the Goddess." They exit at the back of the audience. Curtain.)


### The Clan: An Improvisation

Unlike the preceding play, with its defined roles and dialogue, an improvisation provides no more than a setting, a group of characters who may be nothing more than archetypes, and a situation. From there, the players create the story and dialogue themselves. For **The Clan** the setting is ancient times in a matriarchal society of your choice. The characters may be **Clan Leader, The Shaman, The Artist, The Hunter,** and **The**

**Child,** and the situation the arrival of some mysterious omen of your choice, which seems to affect the creativity or fertility of the women of the clan. Or the characters may draw on Starhawk's typical group types from *Dreaming the Dark*[6] with the situation being a split between two lovers that puts a strain on the cohesion of the group. The basic elements of plot are generally regarded as 1) the situation, 2) a problem to be solved, 3) the solution, and sometimes 4) a denouement, but ritualists should feel free to explore variations. Decide among yourselves who the characters will be, what the problem is, and let your players have some time to identify with their characters, in order to understand their motivations. Then try to "live" the situation, taking whatever time and discussion it takes to solve the problem you have set for yourselves. Improvisation provides a forum for creativity by the actors and for self-exploration by ritualists, and in the case of **The Clan** by experiencing the satisfaction and frustration of matriarchal life and how our society prevents us from re-creating it in our own lives.

As we have seen, there are a wide variety of formulas and tools for the incorporation of our understanding of the sacred nature of sexual energy, and myriad ways to incorporate them into magickal practice. Empowering our magickal work with the strength of the Goddess's own vitality, whatever we as Witches set out to manifest, to change or to mold to our design, will make itself felt and seen in the world with increasing vigor and effectiveness. Through the recognition of the symbolism of female and male divinity in ourselves and using them and an awareness of the Earth's cycles with poetry, song, dance, drama and psychic tools, we infuse our lives, our magick and our planet with fertility, creativity and abundant futures. And we shall as individuals discover that the Rede, the law of return of energy, is truth. The power that we build into our Craft comes back to each of us as joy in our lives, in our relationships, and in deeper, more varied sexual and affectional satisfaction.

[1] Many symbols that we associate with the God have violent connotations (spears, arrows, swords and so forth). I can only encourage you to recall that these have been tools for survival (with the exception of the sword) in hunting societies, and to draw your own conclusions. Perhaps a related vaginal symbol would be a Venus Flytrap or the human imitation of it.

[2] Weinstein, Marion, *Positive Magic: Occult Self-Help*, Custer, Washington: Phoenix Publishing Co., 1980, p. 54.

[3] Robin Fre, "Tyme," on Kay Gardner, *Fishersdaughters*, Even Keel Records, 1986.

[4] Syntonic Research, New York, New York. Available in most record stores.

[5] Gardner, Kay, *A Rainbow Path*, Durham, North Carolina: Ladyslipper, Inc., 1984.

[6] Starhawk, *Dreaming the Dark*, Boston Massachussets: Beacon Press, 1982, pp. 115–128.

# Air, Fire, Water and Earth: Magickal Sex

It doesn't matter whether you first read this section on how to find and foster the magick inherent in your sexuality or the preceding section on the sexuality inherent in your magickal practice. One will heighten your sense of the other. It is important that you read both. Tapping the sacredness of love-making will support the growth of Goddess-consciousness in yourself as a physical, amorous woman and will energize sexual self-exploration through the symbols and trappings of magick. But leaving your sexuality in the realm of the sacred will stunt your growth, make love-making too solemn, or at the very least limit your ceremonial sense of sex to an artificial or rote observance of the Goddess's own physical reality. As a result, you will not be able to completely identify with Her and Her vibrant, erotic qualities. Finding the elements of magick in your daily sex life, whether you are solitary, in a partnership, or simply sexually active will reinforce your own identification with the Goddess and lend insights and enthusiasm to exploring the elements of sex in sacred practice. It will help remind you that the practice of Wicce need not, in fact, be a formal and solemn affair, but one of laughter, passion and joy.

First of all, because you are the Goddess, because you participate as an individual localization of Her on psychic, emotional, intellectual AND physical levels, you are a participant in the fertility and growth that you see all around you. Like Her, you include the God as part of your being, making you a constant reenactment of their love and creativity. The feminine and masculine, two elements of yourself continually interact, in or out of relationships with other women or men. Whether you see it as a balancing of two poles or as the varied coupling of two lovers in your spirit, your feelings, your ideas and your physical body, the harmony is constantly being sung, the love-making going on. This is always true, not only when you are conscious of it, as in ritual or meditation.

The God and Goddess are always trying to come together in you, in everything, in every way. Keeping them apart need not be a problem, for a limited period. We often need to focus on just one aspect in order to nurture it and give it the purest possible expression, in order to affirm it for its own sake and the sake of ultimate balance (what we often call "the pendulum effect"), but a permanent estrangement of the two will cripple both. This is no less true if you are separatist in your politics, exclusively woman-identified in your relationships. You need not relate to individual male humans to achieve balance because the balance is inward, and the elements for it are already there. To insist on rejecting the masculine deity is buying into patriarchy's role for the God: it is like rejecting Jehovah in favor of Satan—you are still a Christian. Central to the revolutionary aspect of Wicce is the reclaiming of matrifocal values and concepts, not simply substituting female for male pronouns and genitalia. Interestingly, it has been my experience that it is not lesbian separatists who neglect to express the spectrum, even though they might voice rejection of the masculine. Rather, it is the woman in a highly dependent relationship with a man or one strongly identifying with patriarchal institutions or religion who surrenders to him or them all the expression of her masculine side, thus starving her feminine side and denying and repressing the Goddess within her. This woman, rather than the separatist, is immersing herself in self-denial.

Being aware that this ever-present love-making is going on between the feminine and masculine divine within you is a first step toward using it creatively, in magickal practice and in sexuality. This is not a balancing act between so-called passive and active forces because those concepts are artificial and polarizing. The energy present is that of creation, pure and simple, of the fact that the interaction between different elements brings about the change, the manifesting of something new. Water lying in a pool is simply water. But water in a pool acted on by the sun's rays creates evaporation and therefore humidity, clouds and rain, the nourishment of life on Earth. Feeling this generative energy within you enhances your sense of effectiveness in ritual, and using sexual symbolism and sex itself can give solid form to the use of that energy. Likewise, looking outside the physical act of love-making to recognize and affirm its sacredness, its participation in divinity, will heighten and nourish sex.

As mentioned in the preceding chapter, sex can be part of ritual itself, even be the heart or purpose of the ritual. Elements of ritual, such as casting a circle, can be added to your "mundane" love-making. (See "Brigid" fantasy below.) You may wish to make love sometimes in your ritual space. In fact, for a couple particularly attuned to the generative force in Wicce, keeping an altar at the head of your bed (which should therefore be at the north—which is beneficial for dreams anyway) is a comfortable and appropriate symbol. Be sure to cast a large enough circle to include all the space you need. Remember, however, that anywhere you make love is a temple to the Goddess.

While sex need not always encompass love, nor love sex, as pleasure and joy are the Goddess's gift as well, many people find that love enhances sex. That's why we call it "lovemaking." Loving yourself is included! The bottom line with the Goddess within is that if you do not love yourself, She will be exceptionally difficult to locate: She will be there, but you will have a hard time finding Her. With a partner or partners love adds a quality of interconnectedness to intimacy. Loving that other, you will find aspects of the body or personality you might not have noticed or felt as strongly without love. The continuation of intimacy brings a greater appreciation of love, and greater comfort and communication. Also, when you make love, you and your partner blend auras and energy centers, eventually taking on parts of each other's. This is the quintessence of the union of Goddess and God, of sex magick. Thus it is quite imperative that your partner be someone you would be happy to BECOME, because to some degree you do just that.

Being together for a long time has its problems too, at least according to our popular culture. Not a few couples have discovered boredom, or interpreted a loss of newness as ennui. Identifying yourselves strongly with magick may help with that. Any sex manual will give you plenty of advice on adding spice to your sex life. Look first to see if all you need is a reminder of what you already have between you. Read your old love letters or look at early photos of yourselves. Then reconsider your relationship in light of its sacredness. Make sure each of you is communicating your desires. Then be adventurous, try new places, new times, new techniques, new tools and new positions. Ask an old married couple with that unmistakeable glow how they have kept it going, and you will discover that boredom is only as big a problem as you allow it to be or give it an excuse to be.

Adding an awareness of magick to your sexual life can be as indirect as recognizing sexuality in your ritual symbolism. Or it can be as direct as embroidering a labyris on your pillow, painting moons and pentagrams on your body with body paint, or using some of the following ideas.

## Spice Up Your Sex Life

Several friends have told me that for them one of the fringe benefits of celebrating the Goddess is the opportunity to play, to dress up, to experiment with jewelry and makeup, to release the little child, the Younger Self. The ultimate effect for many Witches appears to be a general sense of physical freedom. We begin to move more gracefully and assuredly. We dress more brightly and exotically. We're more adventurous. Considering the new public freedom that comes as a bonus of the Wicce experience, think of the possibilities for one's private life!

Wiccean ceremony offers a variety of tools and trappings that can be transferred for use in that other sacred act, sex. In ritual these objects or practices have the purpose of focusing you into an altered state of awareness, through their ties with tradition and through the unconscious. Adding some of these to your sex life can both enhance your sense of the sacredness of making love and help you focus into those associations which liberate inhibited desires.

Anyone who has ever donned clothing to which she is not accustomed, whether it be formal attire or a Halloween costume, has experienced the change of behavior that tends to come with it. Suddenly one feels mature and refined or impish and daring. Many women find that sexy lingerie turns them on sexually, and there is no denying that men's underwear has taken a definitely randy turn. Ritual clothing not only will aid you in ritual but can enhance a role that you are playing in fantasy or sacred drama. Experiment with what sorts of clothing and colors feel sexy to you and/or make your partner's passion more intense. You probably already have a good idea of this from your public clothing. Now look at your ritual robe(s). It is possible that you will be surprised: either they will reflect a more restrained you, or they are the image of the released you. In either case, you may want to find or create new garments for sex play. Drop any notion right now that if you make love in your priestess robe that it will not be "pure" for the next sabbat. You will have imbued it with far more magickal energy than if it hung in your closet for a month-and-a-half.

Some suggestions for creating new clothes: use natural, soft fabrics, including some that are diaphanous or lacy. You needn't be able to sew since long pieces of fabric, like saris, can be wound and draped around your body, or you can perform a "dance of the seven veils" (draping yourself with colorful long scarves and removing them one by one) with seven shorter pieces. Be colorful and concentrate on your special favorites. Use colorful thread or fabric paints to embroider magickal symbols around the neckline, hems, sleeves and loins. Use your intuition to make decisions about length, looseness, adornment and what parts of your body to leave bare. Minoan women wore colorful dresses with ample skirts and tight bodices which were cut away around the breasts to leave them bare. Men can play around with God-like floorlength robes, togas and loincloths. Possible sources for ideas are the artwork of ancient times, books on ancient and medieval costuming, movies, Native American and African clothing, and current pagan literature. Don't neglect headgear: crowns, hair ribbons, circlets, horns, feathers, scarves, headbands and elaborate hairstyles.

Of course, skyclad can be the most erotic of all, but you need not go entirely unadorned. Ritual makeup is especially effective as it can be very subtly suggestive or outright in its sexual messages. There are many types of makeup, from the colored mud you may find in your area (which can be varied further with vegetable dyes) and theatrical greasepaint to edible and inedible body paints sold in sexual aids stores. Watercolor pens can add detailing. One warning: make sure the paint is not indelible—that purple vulva shape on your cheek may be hard to explain to your co-workers tomorrow. Use the makeup to highlight your nipples or buttocks or other especially erogenous spots. Frame your facial features. Draw magickal and sexual symbols on yourself. You might even illustrate a favorite myth or tale all over your body. As an added enticement, if you are sharing love-making, have your partner do all the doodling!

Jewelry is body adornment that is easier both to apply and to remove. There are necklaces, rings, bracelets, armbands, ankle and waist belts, and chains and earrings. Many Pagan jewlers have recently sprung up. There are pentagrams on chains, moon earrings, goddess rings and much more. Another outlet for similar jewelry is the fantasy market, inspired by science fiction/fantasy novels and the fantasy role-playing games. And of course, traditional jewelers usually have many styles of necklaces, bracelets and rings made of precious and semiprecious stones. Particulary appropriate would be red stones, such as garnets and rubies, which relate to the root chakra which is a center of sexual energy. A reference book on healing with gems will give you other ideas.

Since all of these are often quite expensive, an alternative might be imported jewelry, such as bellydance items, costume jewelry such as brightly colored beads, and handmade jewelry. This last offers some of the greatest possibility. You might find it difficult, for instance, to find readymade jewelry to set off your breasts in just the way you wish, but metallic cord, cardboard and aluminum foil can be manipulated into a variety of shapes. You can make beads with paper, glue, poster paints and shellac. Lace made with metallic thread is available in most fabric stores and makes instant "jewelry."

All of these—clothing, makeup and jewelry—can be an integral part of individual or shared sexual fantasies, and are a must for sacred drama and dance. Combine them to personify everything from individual Goddesses and Gods to mythic beings, to animals and plants. Read about and find drawings or sculptures of deities. Imitate or re-create what they wear, such as flowing robes, beaded and feathered headdresses, large crescent necklaces and spirals painted all over your body. Use bright green leotards and tights and a pointed cap to be an elf. Make a lioness costume or simply suggest one with tawny-colored cloth and face makeup.

All the senses have great erotic potential, but for many the sharpest is the sense of smell. This may be a vestige of our pre-human or early human ancestry, when the mate's musk glands aroused and excited us. We have been estranged from our own body scents by the misogynistic values of our society. Ironically, and tragically, to replace them we buy perfumes made of the musk organs of animals who had to be killed to obtain them. Fortunately, our noses are attracted to a wide range of aromas, not merely civet cat musk: flowers, spices and foods. First learn to appreciate your own sweet musk. You can add other scents in the room or on your body. Fill the room with flowers or burn incense. Anoint your body with essential oils, such as patchouli. Most Witchcraft supply shops carry a variety of these oils, including ones specifically associated with love. You can also make them yourself, and you can make rose, orange blossom, and violet waters. Steeping spices and flowers in grain alcohol for several months offers a host of creative possibilities.

Divination tools, such as the tarot, and the symbolism of astrology provide sources both for costuming and magickal symbols and for ideas and suggestions on sexual adventures. The different characters on tarot cards, especially if you have access to several different decks or a pictorial book about the tarot, illustrate costumes and jewelry as well as inspiration for makeup.

The tarot, runestones and I Ching can give specific advice on matters of love and passion. Your horoscope can shed light on your own sexual proclivities and tastes. For instance, an Aries will be direct and energetic, while a Scorpio will tend to surprise you with what she can dredge up from underneath. All these tools will suggest roles for fantasy and sex play.

Sharing the exploration with another or others will not only produce many more ideas and resources, but also will enable you to experiment with a larger number of tools and trappings. Each person can make or buy a few and then share, whether or not you intend to share lovemaking. Sex and the enjoyment of it may or may not be a private act of intimacy, but it is a common blessing, a gift of the Goddess to us all. Most of us will be reticent or embarrassed at first about our ideas or practices, but we all have them. So seek out your friends and correspondents for suggestions and recommendations about clothing, scents and the rest. Try them out, then find the one or many that speak to you individually or as a couple or group. And play!

### Fantasy and Role-playing

"Our sexual experiences are both limited and enhanced by the erotic imagination each of us possesses."[1]

How better to experience your identification with the Goddess in your everyday life than by acting out, in a sense re-living, Her stories? Do you remember how, as a young child, you were able to immerse yourself entirely into pretending, whether playing house, being a cowgirl, a nurse or a princess? (Hopefully, today little girls choose many more roles and thereby experience many more aspects of the Goddess!) For many people a particular role or era speaks most strongly. For me it is Celtic Britain and Ireland, and as a result some aspects of Wicce and stories of the Goddess seem more like a memory than new ideas or information. Perhaps these are other lifetimes or simply the Goddess's recollections coming out in each individual. In either case the ability to pretend is a valuable tool. It shows up in guided meditation and in some rituals. Its powerful link with the child's ability to fully identify with another person or animal is what followers of Faerie traditions would call part of the Younger Self. The key to magick, and to our own memories of childhood's magick, can be the one element that for many of us can help us to overcome self-conscious resistance. Without imagination it is possible that certain insights about the beauty of our bodies, about the Goddess within, about the positive creative nature of sexual symbolism in ritual, might not take place or be able to break down patriarchal society's barriers to self-empowerment. Many adults find that the only way in which they can find the sense of magick through pretending is while immersed in a movie or in sexual fantasy.

Your imagination can teach you things that you could never know without that faculty. It can allow you to empathize with others, to learn their joys and sorrows and to help you understand and care for them better. You can touch the heart of the lonely woman and perhaps understand why she seems to turn others away, or cling to any new friend. You may imagine yourself as a woman with cerebral palsy, confined to a chair and frustrated with others' disinclination to meet your eyes. It can give you the experiences you need to learn to deal with tense situations or to feel more loved. If you are a lonely woman you can imagine yourself part of a close knit circle, not to try to take the place of real human contact but to soften the sharpest edges of loneliness and to experience social situations until you feel more confident to deal with them. If you are a disabled woman, you can imagine freedom of movement, or see your immobile legs as the fish part of a mermaid.

Sexual fantasy, or imagining sexual experiences which involve people or techniques or locations other than a woman might have available in her material life, can be a start for those wishing to re-learn their childhood's capacity to identify. By using Goddess myths or inventing characters from a Goddess worshiping culture, the fantasies might help you along to fuller recognition that you are the Goddess.

This self-empowerment will spread over into your experience of sex as well, heightening its sense of sacredness as well as affirming and freeing your love for your body and sexuality. Start with erotic stories, reading them to yourself or aloud. Then begin to make up your own. Historical novels, myths, fairy tales, fantasy literature will begin to get you started on ideas for fantasies. There are a number of books of women's sexual fantasies available now, as well as on women and sex in general. Put yourself in the Goddess's or heroine's role, and convert or write a love scene for her. Give your imagination lots of room and encouragement: this is entirely YOUR realm; no one can tell you what is normal or healthy in a fantasy. Whatever imagery you dream up, it is exactly that: an image. It is a tool for you to identify with what you are, a physical localization of the Goddess, and as such will grow over the months and years to reflect the happiest, healthiest, most divine you.


Fantasy 1: Mother Earth

(This fantasy is particularly easy to do in a bubble bath or hot tub as the sense of being suspended is beneficial to being a body in space.)

You are the Earth. Your hands and tongue are gentle breezes

that glide along valleys, mountains, plains and seas. Touch and caress each part of the world, stirring it into life and fertility. Begin with the oceans, your mouth and vagina, feeling the heat of creation as sea plants and sea animals flourish and grow. Feel the dolphins and whales swim, leap and dive within you. Comb your fingers through your jungles, the hair on your vulva, under your arms and on your head. It is hot and moist, full of exotic flowers and fruits with pungent smells. Stealthy animals with bright eyes move through the jungle: feel the tiger, the orangutan and the python. Go on to the plains, stroking and tickling your skin wherever it is flat: your back, your forehead, on your chest above your breasts and your stomach above your abdomen. Feel the soil become warm and last year's mulch become fragrant, nourishing food for new growth. Feel the earthworms loosen the soil, and the first seeds germinate. Feel the fields of grasses, grains and wildflowers become green and blossom, swaying in the wind. Feel rabbits and deer scamper. Dip your fingertips into your valleys, between your breasts and buttocks, between your thighs, and between your toes and fingers. Rivers run through them, stretching toward the burgeoning plains. In the gorges between the mountains, goats leap down to find lusher greenery on the banks, and a mother brown bear brings her twins down to catch salmon in a cold rushing stream. Feel the clouds drift across mountaintops, whether ancient rounded mountains or your sharp peaks: your belly, your breasts and your buttocks. They tingle with the last melting snow and with the hardy creatures, tiny white flowers and powerful eagles, that make their home there.

All the Earth is now vibrating, anticipating the burst of life-giving energy, the moment of the Summer Solstice when the Goddess's ecstacy gives energy to a ripening world. As you begin to stroke your vulva, clitoris and vagina, feel your womb, the Earth's core, as it shifts into its most receptive position. It is the opening of the Earth, and the dilation of your vagina responds to the touch of the Goddess, your fingers. As you build toward a climax, feel a chasm open in the Earth, a chasm filled with a huge whirlpool or a spiraling whirlwind. Energy from the sun and the moon, the stars is drawn deep in, in, in to your core. Within, in that center which is unique to each woman, where your orgasms begin or end, the power gathers and builds. As you begin to feel that release, at the point when your body draws itself in in preparation for climax, feel that celestial energy transformed into living things, everything from protozoa to plants to fish, birds, and reptiles, to mammals and humans. Then reverse its direction and begin to spew the ocean of creatures out of you, up into the atmosphere and then down upon all the different parts of your body. They fall like drops of rain and coat you all over. As your contractions slow and cease, the "rain" slows and ceases. Lie still and breathe for a while. Let your hands sweep across your skin again like warm zephyrs ruffling the leaves of trees and the fur of wolves alike.

### Fantasy 2: The Amazon Warrior[2]

You are an Amazon warrior who has been wounded in battle. You feel no pain, but you are barely above consciousness as you lie in a small boat which seems to be adrift. In your dream-like awareness you wonder about where you are and how you got there. You realize that either you were taken from the battlefield and placed in the boat for a mysterious reason, or that you are drifting toward the Afterworld on a magickal boat.

With great effort you lift your head slightly and open your eyes enough to see that you are close to the shore of a fog-shrouded island. You call out faintly. At the sound of your voice a woman steps into view at the shoreline. She watches as you drift inexorably toward her. When the prow of the boat touches the sand, two more women step from behind her and pull it up onto shore. They reach in and gently lift you. The first woman places a cool hand on your burning forehead and a thin sheet of cloth over you, covering you to your chin.

The women carry you toward a small grove of bushes a short distance away and place you on a cushioned bench of some type. You notice that the bushes are hawthorn and that they are in flower. The two bearers go to fetch water and oils as the first woman kneels by your side. She gently begins to remove your armor and the clothing underneath. She tells you that she is Iris and that Hera has sent her to heal your wounds, as you are meant for a great life, a life of wisdom and power in a civilization of women.

The bearers, a black woman and a ruddy-skinned woman with straight black hair, return. They kneel on either side of you as Iris takes her place at your head. She leaves your range of sight for a few minutes as the other two begin to wash you with warm, jasmine-scented water, then to massage you with musky oils. You cannot see Iris, but you hear the snap of a brooch and the swish of linen cloth against skin.

Your body has begun to warm and glow under the ministrations of the dark women. Your curiosity about Iris has distracted you from noticing that their hands have lingered not on your wounds but on your breasts, your belly and the insides of your thighs. As sensation there begins to intensify, your attention is abruptly on them and on your amazement that you can be aroused at a time like this! You begin to sigh and taking your signal, the two women apply lips, tongues and eyelashes where fingers had gone before. You close your eyes in ecstacy.

Suddenly you feel hands gently pressing your thighs apart. You look up to see Iris, who is naked except for a headband with a mysterious design in the middle. She is radiant with light, and your eyes hungrily trace her form, lingering on the fullness as well as places where the flesh of her body is dimpled. She places one knee between yours and leans down, placing her arms on the bench at your sides. Her lips reach down to touch yours, then open to suck lightly on your lower lip. Her tongue darts out, and she draws it down your chin to the hollow of your neck, between your breasts to your navel, then dips for a moment in your vulva to flick your clitoris.

Everywhere she touches you your skin and muscles glow and are suffused with vitality. Your fever increases, but is not like the dangerous flare of fever on the battlefield when you fell. It is more like the feeling of warm quilts around you when, as a child, you lay in bed, sick. It is as if the flame of passion is driving out the flame of illness.

Iris's hands trace your body, alternating faint touches with firm. The two darker women have continued to stroke and massage you. The black woman places her lips on yours: her mouth tastes like honey. The other draws your hand to touch her breast. You feel it firm and heavy in your palm. Iris is pulling her own breasts over you, from collarbone to your knees. She rests her body between your legs, gently spreads your vulva like a fragile rose, and begins to touch and suck and lick. Your hands stray, first to caress her hair, then one to cup the breasts of the black woman, and the other to seek the soft moist folds of the ruddy-skinned woman's labia.

As the four of you make love, your body's vitality grows with your passion. As you near orgasm, the two women begin a soft chant, in a language you do not know but which you seem to understand, hearing a prayer to Aphrodite somewhere inside you. When you climax, all three women rise and take hands, then drop to enclose you in a loving embrace. The energy shared by their bodies and yours simultaneously circles through their arms and pulses outward. Their smiles and soft laughter and sighs fill your senses as you fall into healing sleep.

When you awaken, they are gone. You are alone in a cleft

on a hillside. Your wounds are healed and you smell a faint scent of jasmine on your skin.


## Fantasy 3: The Witch and the Horned One

It is Beltane night, and you are the High Priestess of a coven in Europe in the Dark Ages. All day your village has celebrated the day with feasts and dancing. You alone have stayed on the periphery of the festivities, knowing that your role as leader of your coven will bring you the greatest pleasure of all mortal women.

As night approaches you are happy to feel the warmth of the spring air, with no tinge of frost remaining. The light dims on the fields around you and the young plants in various stages of birth are poking pale green seedlings through rich Earth. The scent in the air is ripe with the growing crops, the pungency of the cattle and ducks, the food and wine still being shared in plenty and the sweaty bodies of coupling villagers.

You have donned your ceremonial cloak with the Goddess's sign on each shoulder. Your priestesses and priests emerge from the darkness on either side of you. Each wears her or his own ceremonial clothing and a grave expression. Silently, the sounds of the villagers growing fainter as you walk away, all thirteen of you proceed in a line to the sacred spot by the pond.

At the pond you form a circle, in the middle of which you build a bonfire. You join hands in the Circle, humming a low tone and stamping your feet on the ground to wake the Mother. A priest hands you an ancient athame, the one that belonged to your grandmother's grandmother's grandmother. The hilt is made of stag horn. You dip the blade into a chalice of wine held up by your sister, who has just been admitted to the coven. The wine was made in ritual fashion, using specially grown grapes and fermented in accordance with the phases of the moon and imbued with the magickal properties of an herb only you know. You take the reddened athame blade and carry it around the outside of the Circle, stopping at the four quarters to sing praise to the elements.

When the Circle is cast, you begin in a low voice to intone the story of Beltane, of the young Goddess who takes to Herself as Lover the young God who was Her Son. You can barely be heard above the crackling of the fire, which has grown higher and higher. The priest who gave you the athame takes it again and places it on the ground before you. Your young sister places the chalice in front of you, but closer to the fire. As you proclaim these two Goddess and God, they stand before each other between blade and cup. She begins to kiss him, and each slides the robe from the other's shoulders. Their hands move around each other's body, and the look of combined anxiety and anticipation which filled both their faces before the ritual begins to fade into passion. The coven watches, chanting low, as the two sink to the ground and make love.

The other coveners turn to one another, women and men, men and men, women and women and sink to the ground. Only you remain standing, the thirteenth member, the odd number. Their sounds fill the air around you as the sip of herbed wine you took from the chalice begins to fill your head with buzzing. The heat of the fire warms the cloth of your robe. You can feel the Mother awakening and feel Her joy in the pleasure which is being shared on this night all over the world. The writhing bodies of untold numbers of Witches, in circles or solitary, on every continent, send shafts of primal energy into the ground, vitalizing the seeds, roots and creatures in the soil and warming the ground so that decaying matter may feed the crops.

As you stare into the fire, a figure appears in its midst. You cannot tell if it is a great stag or a tall man clothed in skins and having a pair of antlers on His head. You gaze into each other's eyes. The heat of the bonfire overwhelms you. As the stag/man nods, you let the robe fall. The heat concentrates in your groin. Outside of time or space he drifts toward you, and you embrace. You know it is Herne, the Horned One, your partner for the sublime lovemaking of the sabbats.

Your lips seek each others' hungrily; your hands press hard against each others' flesh. A rippling sensation spreads down your back muscles. You cannot tell whether you are standing or lying, as the warm air holds you suspended like a soft cushion. You part Herne's legs with your knee, and feel His erection against your belly. He answers your moan of pleasure with a deep, guttural sound. You feel His hands slip from around your body to gently but firmly push your legs apart. His hands caress and probe your vulva. You have fleeting impressions that the mouth which nuzzles your neck and then licks at your breasts is that of a majestic stag. You pass your hands down your own body as you writhe under the ecstacy of the God's touch. Again your attention is momentarily diverted by the notion that you feel light fur instead of moist, smooth skin on your own abdomen.

As you near orgasm one of Herne's hands softly grips one of your hips and guides your body to face away from Him. He enters you from behind, His phallus already lubricated with your own vaginal juices. It fills you and fits you exactly, and you feel the heat of it every centimeter of the length of your throbbing vagina. The poignant energy builds, His phallus and your vaginal muscles exchange the thrilling, breath-taking sweetness of union. Your orgasm starts inside and shoots down your vagina and outward like an arrow, your contractions grabbing Him and pushing Him away simultaneously. You pulse on and on with His thrusts, waves of sweat and chill sweeping over you. You can feel His own energy build inside you and at the moment of His ejaculation you realize that you have both transformed into great harts, and His human gurgle of joy translates to a triumphant stag call.

The mystic world of your coupling flashes bright with golden light and you fall back into nothingness, exhausted and yet full of intense satisfaction. When you open your eyes, your coven surrounds you where you stand in a position of enraptured praise. In a halting voice you join them in a song of thanks to the Goddess who has given the gift of erotic pleasure to you all and whose joining with her Lover, the God, will bring you and all your people a harvest of plenty and security for the winter to come.

*Role-playing in sex* is simply the acting out of a fantasy, usually with one other person. Fantasy is only slightly daunting because you embarrass only the part of you that plays watchdog for the patriarchy, but it takes a little time and sensitivity from yourself and your partner to get over the self-consciousness which is inherent in most adult efforts to pretend. Having an awareness of sex as a sacred act and of this role-playing as a sort of ritual will help immeasurably toward loosening you up. The deeper your identification with the Goddess, the less you will feel that you are behaving oddly or childishly. Ingenuousness is a remarkable trait and should be encouraged in each of us. I will never forget how charmed I was at a young co-worker's stories of how she and her partner, sexually involved and in love since they were both twelve, spun elaborate amorous fantasies and acted them out together.

Role-playing with Goddess consciousness has all the benefits of solitary fantasy with the added benefit of "safe roles" through which to communicate about lovemaking. Start out with minor elements of role-playing if you or your partner is shy. You may, for instance, just take on personae from ancient pre-patriarchal China or suggest that you two pretend that you are in a mossy glen near some standing stones.

Any of the fantasies above can be turned into role-playing scenarios, even "Mother Earth," adding the Sky as a character, male or female, who makes love to the Earth. The following ideas for role-playing can, of course, likewise be turned into fantasies. You may change details in them, of course, including the gender of any characters. In any case, try exchanging roles from time to time, in these or fantasies that you invent. This will be more comfortable for lesbians than heterosexual couples, but the only way to break a useless taboo is by breaking it. Few heterosexuals and gay people *never* fantasize about being the other, and identification with the opposite sex is simply a furthering of identification with both the feminine and masculine deities within each of us.

### Elemental Sex

The following are fantasies using the symbols of the four great elements, Air, Fire, Water, and Earth. Each element has its own special meaning, attributes, and associations in magick, and each has its own possibilities for you to use to get in touch with your sexuality. Read about the elements in other books about magick and improvise freely. Each new aspect of the element will add a new dimension to your pleasure and to your understanding of the element's role in your life and in the Earth. And remember, these fantasies may be shared with others.

### Role-play 1: Air

If you have a tarot deck, remove several cards of the suit of Swords, or Epees. The Sword has its freest movement when being swung through the air. Picture scenes of ceremonial sword dancing: the richly costumed dancers move gracefully, taking big, exaggerated steps or whirling about, all the while swinging their swords about in great arcs and spirals. The swords are bulky and heavy, yet they move with the smooth lightness of banners. Human thoughts and ideas are like this. They may seem ungainly and awkward at times, but once the movement has begun and the resistance mastered, they are as fluid as cloth fluttering in the wind. Our bodies mirror our minds. When we free ourselves of the illusion of gracelessness, we find that our movements are easy and unfettered. We soar.

The best time for an air fantasy is in the early morning, at dawn or soon thereafter. Arrange your love-making space so that when you lie down your heads are in the east. Place incense at the east, something yellow or golden, like sandalwood. Light the incense and a yellow candle. If there is a breeze outside, open the window a bit and let the curtains play in it, or put an electric fan on low speed. Use colors of dawn in the bedclothes: yellow, gold, rose, or peach. You should be skyclad (nude) or wear very sheer, flowing robes, the more imitative of birds' plumage the better. Put on a recording of wind or birdsong. A feather would be a delicious prop.

Relax, then ground and center yourself. Face each other, open your mouths, and begin to breath deeply. Feel the air as it passes over your tongue; taste the incense smoke in the room. Begin to sway gently, shoulders only at first. As the rhythm takes you, begin to move your hands and arms in a fluid gesture in front of you, curling up and over your head, then gracefully down to your sides and somewhat behind. Reach toward your partner, mingling your gesture with his, but do not touch! Smile gently and dreamily.

Slowly begin to stand, and continue your movements, adding your hips, legs and feet, and your neck and head to the dance. Circle each other. Imitate bird walk and wing motions. Take turns imitating each others' movements. Let the air escape from your nostrils and mouth in slow sighing and hissing sounds. When you are ready, slow to a stop, facing each other. Continue to sway. One at a time, take your hands and pass them over your partner's body, never touching the skin but stroking, fondling, caressing in pantomime. Feel free to move or to linger. Feel the warmth on your palms when you pass over some spots and visualize energy emanating from your hand toward each spot. Your partner should focus on the feel of the closeness of your hands and sigh or moan quietly as he feels the warmth or tingling. Then let him take his turn.

Lie down together. Continue to pass your hands over each other. Let them gradually begin to touch your partner's skin very lightly. Imagine yourselves floating on a cloud, or winging delicately together through a spring morning. Keep your caresses and kisses light and tentative. As you progress through lovemaking, move lightly all about your partner's body, touching lightly with fingers, feathers and tongue. The man should mimic the tickling of a feather with his penis, and in coitus he should use light, long strokes, all the while you blow on each others' skin. At the most intense moments, wrap your arms around your partner as if you were folding great wings around him. Afterwards, wrap your wings around each other and doze, feeling buoyed by soft clouds. Wake yourself up as you would on any languid morning, with breakfast together and a long, intimate talk.


### Role-play 2: Fire

Meditate on the Wands, or Batons, in your tarot deck. Think about wood and charcoal, which is made from wood heated under pressure in the absence of air. Wood has many practical uses, but the first by humans was for fire, for warmth. The discovery of the use of fire for heating and cooking was a great leap forward. We became more flexible in our movements, we could live in cooler climates, we could have safer and better tasting food and we could adapt materials found in our environment to make tools and ornament. The fire we used was not that of destruction but of transformation. We used wood for all these purposes and in exchange cleared out fallen wood and brush, responsibly thinning the forest and permitting it to thrive.

The human self is both the wood and the fire. We enflame ourselves with energy, with purpose and with love, and we feed our own fires. We use our uniqueness to fashion our lives and our environment. Passion is our body's fire. We must use it for transformation, too, and the exchange, the consent, must be there. There is great power in passion, the greater still when it is shared.

Wait until the sun is at her highest point. Light a fire in the fireplace, or place red candles all around the room. Place a heatproof bowl at the south and burn woody incense or cedar or pine chips on charcoal in it. Arrange your space so that your heads will also be at the south. Be wildly seductive, with elaborate makeup, lots of colorful jewelry, your hair free and full, and revealing clothing in reds and oranges. Share a light lunch of spicy foods or tropical fruit. If you desire, have vibrators and electric massagers ready. The room should be full of light and bright colors. Put on the sexiest music you can find.

Relax, then ground and center yourself. Sit across from one another, but close, on the bed or floor. Look at each other intently. Focus on your partner's uniqueness, her physical features, her body, her facial expression and her adornment. As you keep in your mind the image of an upright wand, feel the passion for your partner, for those parts of her body, spirit and personality that you find most attractive. As the sexual energy wells up in you, visualize the wand bursting into flame. Clasp each other's hands tightly. When you each sense that your partner's flame is as high as your own, pull each other down and begin to kiss deeply and passionately. Be intense but careful not to hurt. Your passion will transform each other into beings of pure pleasure. Linger long on foreplay to increase the tension. Be noisy: moan, growl, purr and cry out. Do not be content with one orgasm. Afterwards, continue to kiss and stroke. Let the fire die down slowly; don't douse it suddenly. The coals can glow for quite some time. Then get up, clear everything away and go out into the sun.

### Role-play 3: Water

The water suit in the tarot is Cups. Any bowl, rounded cup, goblet, basin, or pool of water will do. In Wiccean tradition the cup is the cauldron, the vessel of change. The prototype of the Arthurian grail was the Cauldron of Cerridwen. The magick was released when a sword was placed in the cauldron. It is a clear symbol of intercourse and fertility.

Cups can receive as well as give. You fill it with water for the express purpose of drinking the water. A lake fills with water from streams and sends it along to rivers and the sea. The sea receives the water and gives it up to the sky, which rains it onto the mountains and streams. There is a constant flow.

Human emotions and psychic energy share this motion and are ruled by the same celestial body, the moon. The monthly changes in our bodies affect our feelings, and the waxing and waning of the moon and her placement in the zodiac determine the best times for magickal working. We share our emotions with others and receive theirs in return. We send out emotions and psychic energy, knowing that they will come back to us. We fill up, like cauldrons, with joy or anger, and pour it back into the world. Our bodies change with the phases of the moon: women and men have hormonal tides, and women menstruate. Both will find that there is a monthly pattern of sexual response. We take food and drink into our bodies and return them to the earth. Women receive seed and give birth to children. We all receive sustenance from the Goddess and return it to Her as love or creative energy.

Pick a twilight with a barely visible moon. If you can make love in or near a pool or lake, good. If not, take a luxurious bath together. Your heads should be in the west; nearby should be a shell with a fruit or flower scented incense. Use light blue candles or if outside, a white candle in a blue glass container. Have ripe, juicy fruits at hand and bottles of juice or wine. If you are not near the sound of running water, play a waterfall or surf recording. Have light flowery colognes ready. Go skyclad or wear swimsuits or light, short robes.

Relax, then ground and center yourself. Move or swim around each other playfully. A water fantasy is a time for laughter, soft, rippling and gleeful. Have fun. Play. Watch the fluidity of each other's body: the grace of limbs, the undulations of muscles, the movement of hair. Concentrate on roundness, looking first at the convex parts. Cup cheeks, chin, shoulders, breasts, fists, abdomen, buttocks, testicles, tip of the penis, knees, calves and heels in your palms. Then stroke fingers and tongue in openings and hollows. Probe and tickle ears, mouth, the hollow of the neck, between breasts, inside elbows, palms, the hollows at waist and in the small of the back, vagina, lightly between the testicles and behind them, behind the knees, and at the ankles and bottom of the feet. Take lightly scented cologne and sprinkle it on each other, or do the same with the water of the pool or tub. Play with putting the convex and concave parts of your bodies together. Be very oral. Tease and tickle. Share fruit and lick the juice off each other's chin. Playfully investigate the activeness of the woman and the receptiveness of the man. After love-making, play tag, or race, or go play in a playground in the moonlight.

# Role-play 4: Earth

Earth is usually symbolized in the tarot with Pentacles, or Coins. In either case, the reference is to the physical and material, or to one's sense of security and groundedness. Many of the cards show people at work or buildings fabricated of heavy stone. The Earth is our mother. Just as we were made out of our mother's body, so everything we touch, build with, eat or breath came from the Earth. The miracle is that every bit, no matter how different, is made up of the same electrons, protons and neutrons, and that they·are all connected in time and space.

The fabric of your own body is made up of the metamorphosed atoms of the humus which fed your mother and you, and which could have been part of a prehistoric sea animal, a mountain in Nepal, a tree in the Amazon or a little girl growing up near Stonehenge. Each has spread its dust to the waters and winds, to be carried around the world. We are all part of the whole, yet each has her own sense of location, of belonging to a space, whether it is a house or a region or just the familiar clothes on her back. Some feel more secure in the midst of a cohesive family or community, some in the sight of a full root cellar and some knowing that nothing holds her down. Our bodies are the most familiar of all. We are at home in our bodies, ideally in complete harmony. We know their abilities, their cycles and their needs. We are our own Earth.

Make your bed up with blankets and quilts in the middle of the night. There should be only one dim candle now. Use musky incenses; the best incense is the smell of the Earth. For this reason an ideal site would be a campsite with the campfire down to coals. Wear Earthy colors like green, brown and ochre. Wear flannels or warm hiking clothes. Be sure your heads are at the north.

Share a late supper of a hearty soup, like lentil, and whole grain bread. While you eat, thank each item in the food separately and picture it growing or living in its accustomed habitat. Look around at the land or the room around you, recognizing the plant, mineral, or animal that each thing is or is made from: plants, wood, metal, wool, even the oil that the synthetics were made from. Relax, then ground and center yourself. Snuggle together under the quilts or inside sleeping bags. Feel each other's solidness, roundness and weight. Hold each other fondly, feeling the safety and security in each other's arms. Mimic the affectionate behavior of animals by nuzzling, licking and purring. Love-making will be slow and deliberate, more focused on affection and closeness than on physical satisfaction, but combine these to feel rooted and permanent. If you are alone, hug your own body and the pillow. Feel cradled. When you are finished, fall asleep in each other's arms.

### Role-play 5: Brigid

This fantasy is a ritual and would be quite appropriate for Imbolc. The purpose for placing all the unlit candles around the bed is that Imbolc, Candlemas, is the ritual for blessing all the candles you expect to use on your altar or for household use for the entire year. Place one specially chosen candle, unlit, in a holder at the head of the bed: this candle is to be set aside to burn at Yule as a symbol of the promise of the waxing light of early February during the darkest day of December.

While the woman is out of the house or in another room the man sets up a bed with its head at the south, in the designated ritual space, using a bedroll, foldout couch or futon. If it is convenient to move the bed or you have a headboard, your bedroom can be the ritual space. Set up an altar at the foot of the bed. Altar candle(s) should be white, the incense should be a light floral. Hide some phallic symbol in the bed but if you use the athame, be careful not to let yourselves be hurt by it. The man should be skyclad or in a loose robe and, unless the woman is inside, she should be fully clothed. The man makes the room as cozy and inviting as possible. A fire in the fireplace would be ideal, but lots of quilts or comforters will do as well. Have a warming snack ready, perhaps mulled wine, cheese and whole grain bread. Turn back the covers of the bed. Dim the lights. Lay all the candles you two expect to use, for ritual and household use for the following year, unlit around the bed. Take one that you have chosen together to be the candle that you will light at Yule as a symbol of the return of the light and place it at the head of the bed in a holder.

Wherever the woman has chosen to be while the man begins the Imbolc ritual, she does something of her own choosing which most speaks to her sense of identification with the Goddess, especially the Goddess Brigid. She will *be* the Goddess throughout this ritual, and the man will be Her new young lover, the God. Both woman and man meditate on being young and new to lovemaking, trying to recapture the feelings of that time. The man marks off the ritual space, being sure the entire bed and all the candles will be included in the magick circle. He might place candles in secure holders at the four directions. He sits at the foot of the bed and faces the altar.

**Man:** *Relax, center and ground. Light incense. Repeat a centering chant many times, such as names of young Gods, or one like the following.*

My light is new burning. I burst forth like buds on a sapling.

*Move to the candle at the east and light it.*

Powers of the East, of Air, of Dawn! Come to your Son, the young God, like at my first sunrise! Bless our union that the Earth may flower and bear fruit for all Her children!

*Move to the candle at the south—not the Yule candle!—and light it.*

*Air, Fire, Water and Earth*

Powers of the South, of Fire, of Noonday! Come to your Son, the young God, who will grow to passionate manhood like you! Bless our union that our Earth may flower and bear fruit for all Her children!

*Move to the candle at the west and light it.*

Powers of the West, of Water, of Twilight! Come to your Son, the young God, who will grow mellow and thoughtful like you! Bless our union that our Earth may flower and bear fruit for all Her children!

*Return to the altar and light the candle on it.*

Powers of the North, of Earth, of Dark of the Night! Come to your Son, the young God, who will find His way back into the Mother at the close of His own day! Bless our union that our Earth may flower and bear fruit for all Her children!

*Invoke the Goddess loud enough for the woman to hear or, if she is outside, go to the front door, consciously taking part of the Circle with you. Call out the door. Needless to say, if you don't think your neighbors could handle this speech you might want to have a signal set up, such as a candle in the window, and you can say the speech later.*

Come, my love, sweet Brigid! She is my young Lady this day, who will know the fullness of womanhood and give grace and bounty to all the world! It is cold and you have looked long for shelter, as the child sun has struggled against the dark to climb higher into the sky. Come in, be warm, be rested!

*The door open, the woman slowly enters the room. The man stays by the door, as if out of sight. He might gently slip her cloak or coat off her shoulders as she enters. It is particularly effective if the woman has elaborate jewelry or clothes on under her cloak, even a tiara on her head to represent the sun's rays. She advances and enters the circle, the man close behind but not in her line of sight.*

**Woman:** *stopping by the bed and taking in all the preparations.*

Long I have travelled in the frozen, barren world. Long have I sought shelter, where I may burn more brightly and begin the Earth's journey to greenness and life. Here is a welcome sight!

*She may make comments on the preparations she sees.*

I bless this Circle and this home with happiness and good fortune!

*She begins to disrobe and pulls back the covers of the bed. At the moment when the athame or other phallic symbol is disclosed, she should pick it up and the man should step to her side. This is NOT a rape story—it is a pleasant surprise for them both and they should greet each other with smiles and laughter. Each should lay hands on the athame, then place it on the altar. At this point, the couple could go into a trance together or begin to make love. I will not interfere with your lovemaking pattern with directions, except for a reminder that you are re-enacting your own first time together.*

**Woman:**    I rise
Spun about by the glowing silk,
The threads of Your love for me.

**Man:**    My tears
Flow down in silvery cascades
To seal Our envelope of joy.

**Woman:**    My hands,
Free from the delicious confinement,
Frame like prayerful hands Your glowing face.

**Man:**    My eyes,
Bound to Yours by the lovebeam gaze,
Fall, only to rise again to their focus.

**Woman:**    We spin
In a spiral of magnetic energy,
Giving off showers of stellar sparkle.

**Man:** Never before
Has the Hand touched Me like this,
Smoothing out a coil of white molten heat
With You
At the core, dispensing the ambrosial fire
Which pulses deep in me, through me.

**Woman:** My joy,
My passion which is Yours alone and forever,
Dear Son, dear Lover, dear Brother,
Radiates in turn to feed Our arcing spirits.

*During lovemaking you will build power quite intensely. At the woman's orgasm, and to a lesser extent the man's, consciously send that energy out to bless the candles about the bed and to the Earth for Her own needs. After you have made love and rested, sit on your bed together. Share the wine, cheese and crackers. Talk about ways in which you each have changed in the past year and what is new in your lives and what you wish to create in the year to come. Light your Yule candle, saying:*

**Woman and Man:** On this Candlemas night, we have given our own passionate fire to feed the flame of the waxing Sun. May this Yule candle bear with it through the Sacred Year that promise of return and of the Mother's blessings on this home and our world. So mote it be!

*Blow out the candle and wrap it in a piece of red cloth, tying it with a gold cord. Dismiss the directions as you normally do and open the Circle, repeating together:*

**Woman and Man:** Merry meet and merry part and merry meet again! May the peace of the Goddess be with you always! Blessed be!

*Kiss.*

*Just as your awareness* of the lusty energy of the Goddess filled your magickal work with vitality and power, so awareness of Her in your own lovemaking brings about joy and wholeness. Look for Her everywhere, not just in your ceremonies. Find Her in the environment and in others, but be sure, first of all, to find Her where She is always very close at hand, in yourself. And give Her gift back again, for energy returns to Her as surely as it comes to each of us, by sharing the affirmation that you have experienced through knowing Her in you. You are the Goddess.

[1] Califia, Pat, *Sapphistry: The Book of Lesbian Sexuality*, Revised Edition, Tallahassee, Florida: Naiad Press, 1983, p. 1.

[2] From a suggested fantasy in the work cited above.

# Afterword: Your Gift to the Goddess

In an earlier chapter we mentioned how certain worshipers of Krishna believe that he experiences all that they do, and that they therefore believe that they have a responsibility to experience great pleasures for his sake. Since a woman's identification with the Goddess is so complete, this is even more true for those who seek Her. A woman's first gift to the Goddess, in exchange for Hers, is to recognize this and to examine her life and to direct it to granting Her this most generous of gifts. At its simplest level, the gift to Her is a woman's love and caring for herself, genuine, forgiving and nurturing.

In her sexual life a woman can give to the Goddess those most basic of needs, honesty and autonomy. She can lift from the Goddess's shoulders any burden of enculturated guilt, restriction or subservience to another person's demands. She can open herself to her own body, learn to accept and enjoy it, and allow it to explore, affirm or reject with its own satisfaction in mind. She can find within herself the natural rhythms of the Earth, that direct tie to the Goddess Herself, and through this connection, she can build and support the awareness of her identity as the Goddess. Every day that a woman is aware is another whole and unrestricted day of experience for the Goddess.

A woman's reverence for her Goddess-self will pour over and

bestow itself on the ones she loves. She need do no more than let it spill over onto them, filling them with the light of her own serenity and with the example of a strong, self-nurturing woman. Whether a relative, lover, or friend, the other will benefit, and the Goddess within that person will be granted the same gift. If they do not refuse her, lovers will have that divinity fed in them, knowingly or unknowingly. This is true even for those who do not know the Goddess. Even those who ascribe to other faiths have within them a hungry divinity which can flourish and grow through the liberation of the body. Partners who know the Goddess but have not experienced Her as the strong and passonate woman She is will learn even more readily how She exists within them. Every localization of the Goddess that the aware woman encourages is thus given the precious gift of life on this planet.

It is likely that the sexually aware woman will know those with whom she can share the gift, by example or by more overt sharing. Simply showing friends how a woman can actualize her self-love, refusing to fall into traps of self-denial or cultural limitations, gives a friend a modicum of strength to realize it within herself. Every man who has such an example in his life is that much closer to finding the Goddess within himself or, at the very least, to learning how to respect the whole person in his woman friend, sister, mother or lover. This empowerment of the woman in every man and woman can lead to greater sexual satisfaction and freedom and less crippling fear of sexuality.

More openly, the woman may return the energy of her Goddess-given sexuality by sharing what she has learned about it through conversation, in Circles, the sharing of this and other books with messages of self-worth and in workshops. I invite and encourage others to explore and write about the Goddess within and Her part in our joy in our own bodies and sexuality.

It is nearly axiomatic in our society that the most liberal of parents will withdraw into doubt and repressive behavior when faced with influencing the sexual actions of her own child. (This child may be a girl or a boy; however it is a societal norm to repress the sexuality of a girl far more than that of a boy. In fact, boys are often encouraged where girls are sheltered.) The reasons are many and complex, mixing the most selfish of desires to control with the most well-meaning and caring of desires to protect. The woman who has found the Goddess within is not exempt and when faced with sharing her affirmation of sexuality with a young daughter may find it hard to remember how much the repression of the Goddess in sexuality and of the sexuality in the Goddess led to her own self-denial, confusion and loss. But she must remember. She must subject herself anew to self-examination to learn the true origin of her impulse to keep her little girl ignorant, naive and "protected."

The woman attuned to the Goddess has a special gift for the world and for her child. She can return to our world the sense of wonder and joy at the beauty and pleasure of our bodies. She can break through Puritanical restrictions as well as mistaken notions of age-appropriate behavior, to allow her daughters and sons to learn that saying "no" to oneself is an autonomous decision based on love and knowledge, and that "no" said to another is as inviolate as the Goddess's law. By teaching children through example and words that their bodies' desires were a gift, and that their own unique shape and color was as much a gift, they can pass on to succeeding generations a stronger and stronger claim to the freedoms of the distant past.

But today's mothers are faced with the dilemma of identifying and differentiating societal pressures from their own intuition. If one chooses to teach one's daughter that her body is her own, will she share it before she can deal with her partner's possible lack of understanding or respect? Will she interpret her autonomy as license for uninformed lovemaking? These and other difficult questions are not simple to answer. The bottom line is to suggest that you trust BOTH your own and your child's intuition, and to provide ample and accurate information about sex, contraception and sexually-transmitted disease, just as you would teach her about nutrition and personal safety. Guard your language for those words which will shade your positive intent with our society's distrust of women's ability to make their own decisions about sex. Whether the subject is menarche, masturbation, same gender love relationships, diet or contraception, your love and confidence will do more than hours of lectures about your child's future. And remember, her future is simply not in your hands. She will grow and learn with your help, but also with the help of great joys and deep sorrows. And she is the Goddess, too.

# Bibliography

The following is a partial list of books to which I am indebted for the development of the ideas expressed in this book.

Barbach, Lonnie. *For Yourself: The Fulfillment of Female Sexuality.* Garden City, New York: Anchor Books, 1975.

——*For Each Other.* New York, New York: New American Library, 1982.

Bethards, Betty. *Sex and Psychic Energy.* Novato, California: Inner Light Foundation, 1977.

Boston Women's Health Collective. *The New Our Bodies, Ourselves.* New York, New York: Simon and Schuster, Inc., 1984.

Bridges, Carol. *The Medicine Woman's Inner Guidebook.* Self-published, 1981. Originally distributed by Earth Nation, P.O. Box 158, Bloomington, Indiana 47402.

Budapest, Z. *The Holy Book of Women's Mysteries, Part 1.* Oakland, California: Susan B. Anthony Coven #1, 1979.

——*The Holy Book of Women's Mysteries, Part 2.* Oakland, California: Susan B. Anthony Coven #1, 1980.

Califia, Pat. *Sapphistry, The Book of Lesbian Sexuality.* Tallahassee, Florida: Naiad Press, 1983.

Chernin, Kim. *The Obsession: On The Tyranny of Slenderness.* New York, New York: Harper and Row, 1981.

Corinne, Tee. *Labiaflowers: A Coloring Book.* Tallahassee, Florida: Naiad Press, 1981.

Dodson, Betty. *Self Love and Orgasm.* Self-published, 1983: write to P. O. Box 1933, Murray Hill Station, New York, NY 10156.

Goldenburg, Naomi. *The Changing of the Gods*. Boston, Massachussetts: Beacon Press.

Hutchinson, Marcia Germaine. *Transforming Body Image: Learning to Love the Body You Have*. Freedom, California: The Crossing Press, 1985.

Iglehart, Hallie. *Woman Spirit*. San Francisco, California: Harper and Row, 1983.

Mariechild, Diane. *Mother Wit: A Feminist Guide to Psychic Development*. Freedom, California: The Crossing Press, 1981.

Monaghan, Patricia. *The Book of Goddesses and Heroines*. St. Paul, Minnesota: Llewellyn Publications, 1990.

Nomadic Sisters. *Loving Women*. Mountain View, California: Nomadic Sisters, 1976.

Rush, Anne Kent. *Moon, Moon*. New York: New York: Random House, 1976.

Scoenfielder, Lisa, and Barb Wieser, eds. *Shadow On A Tightrope: Writings by Women on Fat Oppression*. Iowa City, Iowa: Aunt Lute Book Co., 1983.

Spretnak, Charlene, ed. *The Politics of Women's Spirituality*. Garden City, New York: Anchor Books, 1982.

Starhawk, *The Spiral Dance*. San Francisco, California: Harper and Row, 1979.

——*Dreaming the Dark*. Boston, Massachusetts: Beacon Press, 1982.

Stein, Diane. *The Women's Spirituality Book*. St. Paul, Minnesota: Llewellyn Publications, 1987.

Stone, Merlin. *When God Was A Woman*. New York, New York: Harcourt Brace Jovanovich, 1976.

——*Ancient Mirrors of Womanhood*. Boston, Massachussets: Beacon Press, 1979.

Walker, Barabara. *The Women's Encyclopedia of Myths and Secrets*. San Francisco, California: Harper and Row, 1981.

Weinstein, Marion. *Positive Magic: Occult Self-Help*. Custer, Washington: Phoenix Publishing Co., 1980.

——*Earth Magic: A Dianic Book of Shadows*. Custer, Washington: Earth Magic Books, 1980.

Woods, Margo. *Masturbation, Tantra and Self-Love*. San Diego, California: Mho and Mho Books, 1981.

And a host of periodicals, including:

*Womanspirit Magazine*
(no longer published, but back issues available with an excellent index to all 40 issues available for $13.00)
2000 King Mountain Trail
Sunny Valley, Oregon 97497

*Country Women*
(no longer published)

*Of a Like Mind*
P. O. Box 6021
Madison, Wisconsin 53716

*Sagewoman*
P. O. Box 5130
Santa Cruz, California 95063

*Goddess Rising*
4006–1st NE
Seattle, Washington 98105

*Radiance*
P. O. Box 31703
Oakland, California 94604

Woman-oriented sexual supplies, books and toys:

*Good Vibrations*
3492 22nd St.
San Francisco, California 94110

*Eve's Garden*
119 W. 57th St.
New York, New York 10019

Both stores do both walk-in and mail order sales.

*Nan Hawthorne* lives in the beautiful Pacific Northwest with her partner Jim, their laid back cat Stanzi and a spunky brown gerbil named Cordelia. In the mid-1970s, failing vision brought her to forsake more cerebral pursuits to search inward and find the Goddess within. She considers her life's work to be the development of the Circles of Exchange, a correspondence network for women of spirit, and her writing and speaking on the positive messages Goddess religion has for women in their relationship to their own bodies. Her work has appeared in such feminist publications as *Womanspirit, Sagewoman, Of A Like Mind, Goddess Rising, Asynjur, Bentwood* and *Albatross*. Her goals are to increase awareness of disability issues within the feminist movement and the Craft, to promote a simple and personal approach to ecological concerns, and to someday learn to build fountains.

# Index